Walt and His Park

Phil Gramlich

Theme Park Press
The Happiest Books on Earth
www.ThemeParkPress.com

Editor: Bob McLain
Layout: Artisanal Text
ISBN 978-1-68390-342-0
Printed in the United States of America

Theme Park Press | www.ThemeParkPress.com
Address queries to bob@themeparkpress.com

For my wife, Amy, and my kids, Alexa, Zoey, and Jack. How cool is this?

Contents

Introduction

This isn't an encyclopedia. It's a collection of stories I've put together from primary and secondary sources about the life of Walt Disney and the history of Disneyland. These stories either come from those that personally experienced them, or they were told to them by the people who were there. These are often instances of people recounting personal conversations or meetings they were in with Walt Disney himself. I've heard a lot of stories I chose not to include here because, frankly, key parts either seemed implausible or were directly conflicted by others who were there.

So what's left is a curated oral history of fun, interesting stories that shaped the people, culture, and legacy of some of my favorite places on Earth. I hope you enjoy reading them as much as I enjoyed gathering, writing, and organizing them.

You'll also notice that I purposely left out chapter numbers. That is because I want you to read them in any order you want! These are stand-alone stories that can be read by title, by mood, by length, or you can read them in the order of their presentation. It's your book, do whatever you want with it.

One final note: In some of the stories, I recount conversations for which I wasn't present. Although I'm confident of their accuracy, they are not direct quotes but rephrasings.

Thanks for picking this up!

—Phil

Marceline

"More things of importance happened to me in Marceline than have happened since-or are likely to in the future." These were Walt Disney's words in a letter he wrote to the *Marceline News* in 1938.

Walt Disney's father, Elias Disney, moved his family to a farm in the small town of Marceline, Missouri, when Walt was just four years old. Most of Walt Disney's favorite childhood moments happened in Marceline. Walt sold his first ever drawing to a neighbor in Marceline when he was only seven. On one summer day, he charged all of the kids in the neighborhood a dime to come into the Disney Family barn to watch a "circus." When the kids stepped inside, they realized that the "wild animals" in the circus were a pig, a goat, and the Disney family dog dressed in one of Walt's little sister Ruth's dresses! Flora, Walt's mom, insisted on refunding the kids' money.

The old Disney Family farmhouse in Marceline, Missouri, has been rebuilt and added to over the years.

Then there were the trains. Walt became obsessed with trains during his childhood days on the Marceline farm. His uncle, Mike, was an engineer on the Santa Fe Railroad that would come through Marceline. Uncle Mike had a special toot of the railroad whistle he created just for Walt and his older brother Roy. When they would hear the distant "tooooooooot... toot, toot!" of the engine during the days, they would run to catch up with the train and jump in the slowly-moving cab with their uncle, riding the rest of the way to the Marceline Train Station with him. At night, Walt and Roy would lie in bed together, waiting to hear the train and the familiar toot when they knew Uncle Mike would be passing through. When Walt was 15 years old, he got a job himself aboard the Santa Fe Railroad as a news butcher, selling newspapers, snacks, and cigars to the passengers.

His love of trains is what led Walt to eventually build a backyard railroad, The Carolwood Pacific, on his property on Carolwood Drive in the Holmby Hills section of Los Angeles. When even that wasn't big enough for the kid that once rode the real rails with his Uncle Mike, Walt moved his ideas down the freeway to Anaheim — and a new railroad was built from Walt's dreams.

Walt's "First Drawing"

When Walt Disney was about six years old, he and his kid sister, Ruth, used tar on the ends of sticks to "paint" on the side of the Disney home. When Walt's dad, Elias, discovered his kids' artwork and couldn't remove it from the side of the newly-painted, white farmhouse, he invited his son out to the barn for a "lesson in painting". Sadly, it wasn't the first or last spanking of young Walt's life.

Elias had a brother, Robert Disney, who was married to a woman named Margaret, who Walt and his siblings called Aunt Maggie. Aunt Maggie was one of Walt's favorite relatives and she just happened to visit the Disney Family farm soon after Walt and Ruth's painting session. Maggie mentioned to her brother-in-law that she actually thought some of the paintings that Walt had done on the side of the house were pretty good! She informed Elias that, on her next visit, she planned to bring Walt real art supplies so that he could properly express himself.

Elias told Margaret that no child of his would have time for such foolishness. They lived on a farm, and there was plenty of work to go around, even for a little boy. It was a good thing for Walt that his Aunt Maggie didn't listen to his dad. On her next visit, she brought Walt sketching pencils, a sketch pad, and colored pencils.

At six years old, Walt still hadn't started school. In fact, Elias had insisted that Walt wait until his sister Ruth was old enough to begin school so they could both start the first grade together. Walt's mom, Flora, taught him to read at home around this time. She also helped Walt arrange his day so that he could get through all of his chores in the morning and right after lunch, leaving the rest of his afternoon free for him to meander around the farm, looking for animal subjects to sketch.

Walt would sometimes accompany the Disneys' neighbor, Doc Sherwood, on his rounds around Marceline. Doc was a physician and a family friend, and Walt loved riding next to

Walt Disney's first memory of the Disney Farm in Marceline was that it had a beautiful front yard.

him in his surrey that was led by Doc's big horse, Rupert. On one afternoon, Walt brought along his new pencil and sketch book, keeping it hidden under his jacket. When Doc would go into each home to check on each patient, Walt would find an animal subject and sketch it, always being sure to hide the pencil and pad under his jacket when he saw Doc heading back to the surrey. Walt was a shy kid, and while his mom and his Aunt Maggie would praise him for his drawings, he still didn't have the confidence to let anyone else see them!

After their final stop of the day, Walt held the horse's reins while Doc filled out his report on his latest patient. When Doc's pencil tip broke, he looked at Walt and said (I'm paraphrasing...always paraphrasing), 'Walter, can I borrow your pencil? And while you're at it, why don't you show me what you've been drawing all afternoon?'" Walt sheepishly reached into his jacket and pulled out his sketchbook to show Doc a drawing of the last patient's dog asleep in the sun, a scene he had captured on his pad while waiting for Doc to return. 'That's very, very good Walter,' Doc told him. Then he asked Walt, 'Would you draw a picture of my horse for me?' An excited Walt enthusiastically agreed!

Doc Sherwood stood and held Rupert's reins while Walt sketched his prize stallion. Walt later said that the Doc must've held that horse there for an hour, giving Walt plenty of time to get all of the details absolutely right. When he was finished, Doc took the drawing and told Walt how much he loved it. Then he told Walt, "I believe a man should be paid for his services. Not just in hams and bushels of corn, the way I do sometimes, but in good, cold cash. That's why I'm going to pay you five cents for this drawing." At just six years old, Walt Disney, the artist, had made his first sale.

The Owl

One summer evening in 1908, seven-year-old Walt Disney was wandering around the family farm in Marceline, Missouri, all alone. All of the adults and Walt's siblings were busy doing other things, so Walt, like any other curious kid his age, was looking for something interesting to do. He spotted a big owl on a fence by the Disney's apple trees and decided to follow it into the orchard.

Walt kept following the owl through the trees until it landed on a branch that was low enough for him to reach out and touch. He inched closer and closer to the owl until, finally, his childhood excitement and exuberance got the best of him and he suddenly reached out and grabbed the owl by the legs!

Of course, being a wild animal, the owl had zero interest in being accosted by a human being! The owl scratched and clawed at Walt, trying to free itself from Walt's hands. Walt instinctively threw the owl to the ground, then stepped on it, killing it.

Walt was devastated. He had nightmares about that moment and about menacing owls for the rest of his life. Evidence of his owl issues can be seen throughout

Imagine young Walt and his siblings watching the sun come down while lying in the shade of the family barn.

the animated films he made, including the big, dark barn owl from "The Old Mill". That guy has always freaked me out for some reason, and I think of Walt's owl every time I see him now! In an article the late Disney Historian, Jim Korkis, wrote for Mouse Planet, he included this quote from Walt about the incident: "I could see that darn owl in my dreams, you know? But I was just so excited. I didn't want him. I didn't want to kill him. But when he began to claw and everything else, I got so excited I threw him on the ground and stomped on him, you know? And I killed him. I didn't want to kill him. I didn't have it in my mind at all. And I don't know yet why I wanted to have that owl. It was just...I could catch him, you know? He was on a low limb there."

Homemade Butter and Rubber Bladders

When the Disneys were still trying to make ends meet in Marceline, before Elias sold the family farm and moved the family to Kansas City, Missouri, the family relied on the door-to-door sales of Flora Disney's homemade butter to neighbors and the townspeople of Marceline for extra cash. Elias would have milk delivered weekly to Kansas City by train, and Walt and his brother Roy were tasked with going to the train station to pick it up. Door-to-door butter sales were still a big part of the Disney family income when Elias, Flora, Walt, and his siblings, Roy and Ruth, moved to Kansas City in the summer of 1910. Times were tough and money was tight, so Elias demanded that his wife only use the smallest amount of butter for the family's bread at dinner. Butter equalled cash in his world, so Elias used none. Flora did as she was told, and only added the slightest bit of butter to each child's bread. Of course, what Elias did not see, was that she had already heavily buttered each piece of bread for her children, then placed them butter-side-down on their plates. Elias never caught on, and Walt, Roy, and Ruth always had plenty of butter to enjoy!

Walt and his mom were very, very close and he, without a doubt, inherited his fearless, fun, and feisty personality from her. Walt was always interested in magic and practical jokes, and when he was a tween, he bought a rubber bladder with a hose and a squeeze bulb at the end of the hose. It was a magic trick that could be hidden under a tablecloth. When a plate was placed on top of it, the trickster could make the plate rise and fall with the little squeeze bulb. Walt tricked Flora with it one night while she was preparing dinner and she got a kick out of it! Flora excitedly told Walt something like, 'I'm going to use this to trick your father!'

Walt's dad, Elias, was not very fun and did not love jokes, but he was certainly feisty and fearless! When he sat down to dinner that night, lowered his head and slurped a spoonful of soup from his bowl, Flora squeezed the bulb so that Elias's plate and soup bowl rose and fell! Flora and the kids started cracking up laughing, but Elias didn't even notice it. So she did it again. And again. With every spoonful of soup, with every slurp, the bowl and plate would rise and fall. Flora laughed so hard that she was shaking the table, but Elias STILL didn't catch on! He said something like, 'Flora, why are you being so silly?! I've never seen you act this silly in all of our years together!' Flora couldn't stop laughing. She had to go into the bedroom to lie down and catch her breath. Walt Disney was the consummate gag man, just like his mom was the consummate gag woman!

Walt followed his mom up and down the streets in Marceline, selling butter door to door.

The Two Walts

Walt Disney was an average student in elementary school. He would often daydream, staring out the window instead of completing his teachers' assignments on time. Sometimes he'd even fall asleep in class, a byproduct of having to get up before dawn each morning to deliver hundreds of newspapers for his taskmaster of a father. Walt never resented his dad, Elias, for his ways, though. He credited his dad for his own toughness and reserve. It was more than toughness, however. Elias Disney was a bit of an unhappy person. He didn't enjoy life as much as most. While Walt's mom, Flora, was quick to laugh, joke around with her children, and encourage imagination, Elias did none of those things. He was devout in his religion. He did not drink. He did not smoke. He also did not have time or patience for foolishness.

In the fifth grade, on Abraham Lincoln's birthday, Walt used shoe polish to give himself a black beard and prominent mole, fashioned cardboard around his dad's old hat to convert it to a stovepipe, and wore his dad's overcoat, in order to mimic his favorite president. When he got to school that day, he proudly stood up in front of his class and, in his best Lincoln impression, delivered a perfect Gettysburg Address! His teacher was so impressed that she sent for the principal, who was so impressed that he marched Walt around from classroom to classroom, where he repeated his act for the entire school!

Elias was not interested in Walt's passion for entertaining and making people happy. He discouraged Walt from performing. Walt had a best friend growing up in Kansas City, a classmate also named Walt Pfeiffer. Walt Pfeiffer's family, on the other hand, was a big, loving, German family with a piano in the living room and music always in the air. Walt would often spend evenings with the Pfeiffers as a kid, eating German staples for dinner and singing songs around the piano

Walt's childhood friend Walt Pfeiffer would help Walt sneak out of the Disney family home on Bellefontaine Avenue.

with the family. The Pfeiffers' home might've even been where Walt first discovered his love of hot dogs!

In the fifth grade, Walt and Walt Pfeiffer entered a school talent contest at the Benton Grammar School in Kansas City. The boys put on a skit where they asked for a volunteer from the audience of their fellow students. They chose a boy to come up on stage so that the two Walts could take a photograph of him using their "camera". When the poor kid sat down, Walt pointed the trick camera at him, clicked the shutter, and water sprayed out across the stage and onto the volunteer. The crowd laughed as Walt Disney opened the camera and removed the "photograph" to give to the volunteer, which was a cartoon that Walt had drawn before the act!

The Two Walts, as they became known, went on to perform their sketch comedy acts in vaudeville theaters across Kansas City! Walt Pfeiffer would come to Walt's bedroom window at night to help him sneak out for their performances. It was a foolproof plan, really. Elias never checked on his children after they went to bed and Flora, who supported Walt and his imagination and creativity, would've let him off with a slap on the wrist if she had found out on her own.

Walt Becomes Charlie Chaplin

Walt Disney's dad, Elias, was a penny-pinching kind of guy. He didn't believe in buying many toys for his children or investing in anything other than their education. Walt's pal, Walt Pfeiffer's dad, on the other hand, spent money more freely on his family and children, would take them to local shows and events, and would help his son and his friends see vaudeville shows at local theaters during the Sunday matinees.

One Sunday, the Two Walts and some other friends watched a silent film starring a young actor named Charlie Chaplin. They all laughed and hollered through the film, and when they got outside into the sunlight, Walt Disney shrugged and told his pals with a grin, "I can do that!" When they all asked what he could do, Walt responded with, "Act like Charlie Chaplin. I just know it. I'll prove it to you next Sunday."

Walt knew that his parents wouldn't be home for quite a while with all of their church activities, so he had plenty of time alone to execute his plan when he made it back to the Disney house at 3028 Bellefontaine Avenue. He went right to his father's closet and found the perfect oversized shirt, pair of pants, and jacket to wear. Then he slipped into his dad's dress shoes that were a few sizes too big. He checked himself out in the mirror and he looked the part, but something was missing. Of course, he forgot Chaplin's mustache! Walt walked into the kitchen and dug his index finger in behind the stove, covering it with soot. He went back to the bathroom and used his sooty finger to draw the perfect Charlie Chaplin stash on his upper lip!

Once the look was complete, Walt took a kitchen knife, went out to the backyard, and cut a fallen branch from a tree into a perfect cane. He then stood in front of the full-length mirror in his parents' bedroom and couldn't believe when he saw Charlie Chaplin staring right back at him! For the next hour, Walt practiced Chaplin's waddle and movements in front of the mirror while keeping an eye on the clock, making sure to clean everything up and hide the evidence before his parents arrived home.

For the next week, Walt practiced his Chaplin routine each time he was alone in the house. He would rehearse every one of Chaplin's jokes that he remembered, again and again. He even purchased a paper derby hat at a nearby novelty store to complete his look! When Sunday came, Walt invited Walt Pfieffer and his other friends to the Disney home for his performance.

Walt walked into the room and went right into Chaplin's routines: waddling, duckwalking across the floor, dropping his hat and kicking it across the room, kick by kick, as he bent to pick it up, etc. His friends all exploded with laughter! "That's great Walt," one of them said. "You know what? They're having a Charlie Chaplin contest at the Rialto Theater next Saturday. You ought to enter it. I bet you'd win!" Walt did enter, and he did win! The prize was $2 and fourteen year old Walt Disney had his very first, but certainly not his last, personal award!

Walt's New Boots

It was the winter of 1916 and fifteen-year-old Walt Disney was, insanely, working multiple jobs around his school schedule. Walt would get up at 3:30 each morning to deliver newspapers for his father, Elias, then head to school. On his lunch break, Walt would sweep out the interior of a nearby drugstore in exchange for a hot meal from the drugstore owner. After school, Walt would sometimes deliver prescriptions from the pharmacist by foot to the elderly and others who couldn't make it out to the store, which was the only job he actually received money for. Then, Walt would deliver the evening newspapers for his dad and try to catch his friends at the neighborhood soda fountain before heading home for the evening, having dinner, going to bed, and doing it all again the next day.

On one particular late winter afternoon, Walt had finished his paper route and was jogging across a Kansas City Street to catch up with his friends when he spotted a chunk of ice lying in the street. Just being a kid, Walt gave it a good kick with his new leather boots (a Christmas gift from his parents) and all of a sudden nearly passed out in pain! Screaming, he looked down at his foot and saw that a horseshoe nail that had been frozen in that ice was now sticking through his boot and into his foot! Worse than that, the ice was still frozen to the street, which froze Walt in place, in excruciating pain.

Walt screamed and cried for help, but the sounds of a busy city afternoon drowned out his cries. Finally, after what seemed like an eternity, a man stopped to help. He chipped the ice away, allowing Walt to move his foot, then helped Walt up onto his horse-drawn wagon to take him to a local doctor. The doctor told Walt that he had nothing to help with the pain he was about to feel, had two men in the office hold Walt down, and pulled the nail out of his foot with a pair of pliers! (Phil here...I had trouble telling this story because this part makes me want to pass out with queasiness...so, moving on!)

The doctor gave Walt the appropriate shots to make sure he wouldn't lose his foot, then told him that he had to stay off of it for a couple of weeks. It might've been the first two week break Walt had ever had in his young life. He returned home to recover and spent those two weeks drawing and thinking about what his future might hold. I'm sure Elias was quite upset that he lost his free labor for a couple of weeks, but that break provided young Walt with the time he needed to begin to dream of his life as a successful cartoonist!

Riding the Rails

In the summer of 1916, when Walt Disney was fifteen years old, he took a summer job as a news butcher on the Santa Fe Railroad. If you're not familiar with the term, news butchers were young men in uniform who would walk the aisles of the commuter cars, selling things like magazines, peanuts, candy, apples, soda, and cigars to the Santa Fe passengers. This was the absolute dream job for a train-crazy kid like Walt, and he was thrilled to ride the rails every day!

In an article for *Railroad Magazine* in 1965, Walt wrote, "I felt very important wearing a neat blue serge uniform with brass buttons, a peaked cap, and a shiny badge in my lapel. As the train rolled into one station after another I stood beside the conductor on the car steps to enjoy the envious stares of youngsters waiting on the platform."

Of course, the summer wasn't all sunshine and smiles, and young Walt ran into his fair share of issues. As a matter of fact, on his very first day of work, Walt loaded up his merchandise hamper with as much as he could fit and got himself set up on the train before it took off at 4am. That day, the train took two extra commuter cars, a fact that Walt was not aware of. He sold out of all of his soda quite early due to the morning's heat, and he figured he'd go back to get the empty glass bottles from all of the cars later when his shift had ended (Walt was responsible for returning the bottles to retain his deposit). Well, the train left those two extra cars behind when it made its way back to Kansas City, and Walt's first day of work ended up actually costing him money!

One morning Walt found out his train would be heading to Pueblo, Colorado. The plan was for the train to stop overnight in Pueblo and return the following day, so Walt would need a place to sleep for the night. An older news butcher gave Walt a business card and told him, "Bub, this will get you into a good hotel in Pueblo. You'll like it."

Walt was pretty tired when he got to the hotel in Pueblo. Walking up to the front door, he thought to himself that it sure didn't look much like any hotel he'd ever seen. He knocked on the door anyway, and a woman answered and told Walt to come on in and to make himself comfortable. Walt walked through the front room and could hear a piano being played somewhere in a different room. "Let me get you a beer, son," the lady who answered the door told him. Again, Walt was fifteen. While Walt's new friend was gone, a gentleman and a young lady came walking down the stairs, arms around one another. All of a sudden, Walt realized what kind of house he was in, and he snuck out the door! Walt later told his daughter, Diane, "I was just a kid but I caught on. When I got through the door, I broke into a run!"

Walt's fascination with trains only grew once he worked as a news butcher on the railroad.

A Good Kick in the Teeth

In 1919, eighteen-year-old Walt Disney, fresh out of the Ambulance Corps and a year in France, moved to Kansas City, Missouri, with hopes of becoming a newspaper cartoonist. He secured a job at the Pesman-Rubin Commercial Art Studio where he met another young, aspiring artist by the name of Ubbe Iwerks. After getting to know one another and becoming friends, Walt and Ubbe figured that they could have a lot more freedom to create and grow as artists if they formed their own studio, so they went into business for themselves. Walt Disney, the entrepreneur, was born.

Walt and Ubbe needed a name for their new business venture. When they discovered that the name Disney-Iwerks sounded like an optometrist, they went with Iwerks-Disney Commercial Artists instead. Unfortunately, young Walt and Ubbe knew nothing about running a business, and the company went under in a month. The two friends then took jobs at the Kansas City Slide Company, and it was while working there that Walt discovered animation for the first time. He quickly learned everything he could about what went into animation from the artists at the company, and went to the library to borrow books on the subject to teach himself as much as he could!

With animation as his new obsession, Walt believed that he could open and operate his own animation studio. While still working his day job (at the newly renamed KC Film Ad Company), Walt created a series of animations called Newman Laugh-O-Grams: advertisements that were played on the big screen before silent films. This venture started out successfully, and Walt accepted $15,000 from backers to incorporate Laugh-O-Gram Films, Inc. He hired his friend Ubbe Iwerks and a few other artists to come along for the ride.

As I had mentioned earlier in the story, unfortunately Walt was not yet a shrewd businessman. He signed some bad deals with some not-so-trustworthy people, and he and his artists were never fully compensated for their Laugh-O-Grams. They actually only received about ten percent of what their contract promised. Walt tried to keep the business afloat for as long as he could, even moving out of his room at a local boarding house. He would sleep on the couch at Laugh-O-Gram and take a shower once or twice per week at a city bath house. For food, Walt would eat on credit at the Greek restaurant that was on the first floor below his second floor studio. None of the saving and scrimping helped.

Walt did find an honorable client in Kansas City, though: a dentist named Dr. Thomas McCrum. Dr. McCrum and Walt agreed on a fee of $500 for a short film that would teach young children how to take care of their teeth. The dentist was a member of The Deener Dental Institute, and they would be footing the bill for the film's production. One evening, Dr. McCrum called Walt at the studio and told him that the institute had sent him the check, and he was ready for Walt to come on over and sign the deal for the film. Walt told Dr. McCrum that he would love to, but would not be able to come by. When the dentist asked why, Walt said, "I haven't any shoes. They were falling apart and I left them at the shoemaker's. He won't let me have them until I dig up a dollar and a half."

Dr. McCrum told Walt to hold on, and he'd be right over. When he arrived, he and Walt sat and hammered out the fine print for the short film, which became "Tommy Tucker's Tooth". Walt delivered the film on time and you can still watch it on YouTube! When Walt's daughter, Diane Disney Miller, wrote about this story for "The Saturday Evening Post", she said, "If you wonder how Dad got home from that shoemaker's after leaving his only pair of shoes there, the answer is that the shop was under the Laugh-O-Gram studio, next to the Greek restaurant, Dad walked out of the shop and upstairs in his sock feet."

Of course, not even a successful film could save Laugh-O-Gram from its creditors, and the business went bankrupt in 1923. Walt Disney was undaunted, even as he watched repo men remove everything from his former place of business. He was able to keep a camera that he had owned prior to his start of Laugh-O-Gram, and he worked around Kansas City as a freelance baby photographer for a while, raising enough money to purchase a train ticket to Los Angeles. I've mentioned this in stories before, but a nearly-broke Walt went to the train station in Kansas City and purchased a first class ticket. In his possession he had a faux leather suitcase (made of cardboard), his art supplies, and $40. Like the song says out in Disney California Adventure, he went out there with a "suitcase and a dream."

Walt's Laugh-O-Gram Studio was on the second floor of this building, the McConahay Building at 1127 East 31st in Kansas City, Missouri. A Greek restaurant was on the first floor when Walt and his artists were tenants. The building is being restored to its heyday as this book is being written.

Walt's Home Life & the Red Cross

Walt Disney's dad, Elias, was a difficult man. I struggled for a word to use there, actually, because difficult doesn't seem like it really covers it. Walt didn't say a negative thing about his father and respected him and maybe even adored him, but Elias's treatment of his children would fall under the word abusive by today's standards. Walt's two oldest brothers, Herbert and Raymond, left the Disney family home one night and never moved back due to Elias's treatment of the family. Roy O. Disney, Walt's closest sibling and friend, followed in his older brothers' footsteps, leaving for Kansas City in the middle of the night one night, telling Walt and their younger sister Ruth that he was tired of Elias's ways.

When Walt turned sixteen years old, he wanted out as well. He first tried to join the army, but at 16 he was too young. He found out that the American Red Cross was accepting seventeen year olds to serve as ambulance drivers in France and, wanting to serve his country, he asked his parents to sign a form saying he was seventeen and he could go. Elias absolutely refused. He told his wife, Walt's mother Flora, that she would have to forge his name if she wanted Walt to go. Flora surprised Walt by saying she would. She told her husband that she had already lost three sons in the middle of the night, at least if she signed this paper, she'd know where Walt was. There was a problem, though! Flora wrote Walt's actual date of birth down on the paper, December 5, 1901. It was Walt who, with the quick flick of a pen, made himself a year older!

Walt left Chicago behind and was off to France. One of the other young men Walt worked with in the Red Cross was Ray Kroc, who went on to find a little burger joint that he franchised around the world, called McDonald's. Ray and the other guys thought Walt was a "strange duck" because, when all the boys would go out hunting for girls, Walt would stay home, drawing cartoons. Walt and a friend would collect the helmets of German soldiers and Walt would paint elaborate German sniper camouflage on the helmets. They would make them look battle worn, shellac them, and then sell them to American soldiers who were being sent home as souvenirs. Walt made good money doing this and would send it home to his parents with instructions to get his sister, Ruth, a new watch, and to put the rest in the bank. He wasn't there long when the armistice was signed, officially putting an end to the first World War.

When Walt returned home to Chicago, Elias had a good job lined up for him at the O'Zell Jelly Factory, which Elias had invested in. Walt told his parents that he wouldn't be staying in Chicago and wouldn't be working at the factory. He was moving to Kansas City to become a newspaper cartoonist. His time overseas, where he made good money from painting camouflage on helmets and crosses on jackets, had given him even more confidence that a career in cartooning was in his future.

And this part, I couldn't figure out where to put it in the story because it's funny but the rest of the story was kind

Memorabilia and coins from France after World War I,
saved in this green bag by Walt for his entire life.

of serious. I'm just tacking it on here! When Walt returned home from France, that night he showed his mom, Flora, a tiny box that he was saving as a "battlefield memento." He slowly opened the box so his mom could peer inside, and Flora screamed when she saw a severed finger in the little box! Turns out, it was Walt's thumb, covered in iodine, and stuck up through the bottom of the box. Even at 17 years old, Walt was an incredible gag man!

Walt drove a truck similar to this one during his time with the Red Cross in France.

Kansas City

Walt Disney often spoke glowingly about his childhood years
in Marceline, Missouri. From the ages of five until ten, Walt
and his family lived on a farm located at 119 West Broadway
Street. It was an idyllic five years for Walt and his younger
sister Ruth, especially. Ruth (or Ruthie, as Walt would call her;
those nicknames started early) would tag along with her older
brother often, going swimming, fishing, and dreaming under
a big old cottonwood tree on the family's property.

They would lie in the cool shade under that tree and Walt
would tell Ruth stories and draw pictures of the animals they'd
see. A neighboring farm had a prized bull in a large, fenced-in
field. On their walks back to the Disney farm, it was much
faster for Walt and Ruth to cut across that field than it was to
walk around it, and so the two would often narrowly escape
being trampled by an angry, charging bull!

Walt's dad, Elias, was a serial entrepreneur with a string of
failures to his name. When his health became poor in 1911,
Elias sold the farm and everything that went with it and
moved the family to Kansas City, Missouri. Walt watched as
his favorite animals, more like pets or even friends to him,
were auctioned to the highest bidder. He later said that he
cried as they left the farm that day. Sadly, Walt's childhood
basically ended when Elias sold that farm. When they arrived
in Kansas City, Elias purchased a paper route, and made Walt
and his brother, Roy, get up every morning at 3:30am to deliver
newspapers to the more than 700 subscribers on that route.

Blistering summer suns, tall snowdrifts in the winter, it
didn't matter, Walt and Roy were out delivering newspapers.
Later in life, Walt would say that he enjoyed delivering papers
to the apartment buildings the most, especially in the winter.
There he could lie down on a floor in one of the hallways and
take little naps before heading off to school. For six years, Walt
delivered newspapers in Kansas City. He was never paid a dime

by his father and would often have nightmares as an adult that he was fighting through those giant Kansas City snowfalls. It's really no wonder that Walt wanted to run away to the Red Cross at just sixteen years old.

When Walt returned to his family's home in Chicago after his travels with the Red Cross in 1917, he was no longer that slight newspaper delivery boy that he was when he had left. Walt was about 5'10" and 165 pounds by that time, broad shouldered and strong. He had new ideas about the world and his life that Elias did not agree with. He also had no interest in returning to the life of his father or following in his footsteps. Elias had secured a decent job for Walt at the O'Zell Jelly Factory, another money-making, entrepreneurial effort by Elias that would eventually fall flat. Walt told his parents that he was moving to Kansas City to become a newspaper cartoonist and, while it wasn't all glitz and glamor from this point on for Walt, at least he was his own man. Walt moved to Kansas City in October of 1919 where he took a job with the Pesmen-Rubin Commercial Art Studio, where he met a fellow 18 year old artist named Ubbe Iwerks.

Walt's father, Elias Disney, built a garage in the rear of the home that still stands today. That garage was where Walt first experimented and worked with animation.

A Suitcase and a Dream

In 1923, Walt Disney, Ub Iwerks, and their staff were working on their first Alice Comedy, a ten minute one reel short film that blended live action with animation titled *Alice's Wonderland* at their Laugh-O-Gram Studio in Kansas City, Missouri. Unfortunately, the work on the film bankrupted Walt's first studio.

Of course, we all know now that Walt did not give up. He worked around Kansas City as a freelance photographer for a bit, earning enough money to buy himself a one-way, first class train ticket to Los Angeles, California. That's right, first class. Walt's coat and pants didn't match, he had a cardboard suitcase and only $40 in his pocket, but he made sure to arrive in L.A. in style!

Walt rented a room from his Uncle, Robert Disney, on Kingswell Avenue in Los Angeles, and had plans to become a director in Hollywood. When that didn't work out after some trying, he decided to go back into animation. Walt wrote to cartoon distributor Margaret Winkler (a producer of Felix the Cat cartoons),

Walt arrived in Los Angeles with a cardboard suitcase, $40 in his pocket, and dreams of making it big in Hollywood.

telling her that he was setting up a new cartoon studio in the Los Angeles area and that she should set up a screening of *Alice's Wonderland*. After viewing the still-unfinished film, Winkler telegraphed Walt on October 15, 1923, offering him a contract for his Alice Comedies.

Walt's older brother, Roy O. Disney, was recovering from tuberculosis in a veteran's hospital nearby. The twenty-two-year-old Walt came crashing through Roy's hospital room screen door later that night (Roy was in a screened-in, outdoor room for his TB), telegram in hand, begging his brother to join him in a new business partnership. Roy signed himself out of the hospital the next morning, the same day that Walt signed the contract that started the Disney Brothers Studio.

The cardboard suitcase and $40 yet buying the one-way, first class ticket is so cool. You don't hear people call Walt cool a lot, but that really does speak to the kind of guy he was, even at 22. He wasn't coming back to Kansas City. He had already moved on.

The Meet Cute

Lillian Bounds was a young lady looking for a job when she arrived in Los Angeles in 1923. A friend, Kathleen Dollard, told her about a couple of young guys from Kansas City who had just opened a cartoon studio not too far from where Lillian was living. They were looking for a young lady to act as their secretary and ink the cartoons. Kathleen warned Lillian not to fall for the boss, but the boss, apparently, wasn't told the same thing. He fell for Lillian almost immediately. In the Walt Disney Family Museum, there are all kinds of listening stations set up throughout each gallery with Walt's family and friends telling stories that you can listen to. Diane Disney Miller, Walt and Lillian's daughter, is the voice you hear on many of the recordings. I don't have the quote, but she talked about how Walt would often drive the ink and paint girls home after work. Lillian lived closer to the studio, but Walt would always drop the other girl off first so that he could spend more time with Lillian each night.

Walt and Lillian were married on July 13, 1925 in Nez Perce County, Idaho. They honeymooned at Mount Rainier in Washington and bought their first home in Los Angeles shortly after. One they moved in, Walt started bugging Lilly to get a dog. Lilly didn't want one but that certainly didn't stop Walt from continuing to ask. He bought a book on dogs and would read it often, showing Lilly the different breeds and trying to figure out which one she might let him get away with. Finally, she settled on a Chow. Walt bought a chow puppy the day after Lilly gave the okay, but he kept the dog a secret until Christmas Eve.

Walt and Lilly were celebrating Christmas Eve with family at their new home. Walt hid the puppy in a hatbox with a big bow on top when no one was watching and made a big deal of picking up the hatbox from under the tree and giving it to Lilly. At first, Lilly was a little puzzled because Walt knew that she absolutely did not like anyone picking out hats for her. Then, when the hatbox lid popped up a bit and the little puppy's head peeked out, she screamed!

The New Suit

Walt Disney would always offer to drive his ink and paint girls, Kathleen Dollard and Lillian Bounds, home once their work days had ended. Lillian lived closer to the Disney Brothers Studio so, at first, Walt would drop her off first, then Kathleen second. After he started developing feelings for Lillian, he started dropping Kathleen off first, just so he could spend a little more time with the object of his affection.

One evening, when Walt had walked Lilly to her front door after work wearing the same old clothes he wore a couple times each week, he asked her, "Lilly, if I bought a new suit, would you invite me in to meet your family?" Lillian was living in Los Angeles with her sister and seven-year-old niece. Lilly said she would and asked Walt if he'd like to come

Maybe Walt had a suit in mind like the one he drew here, a few years prior.

in at that moment. Walt declined, saying he needed the new suit to make the right impression.

The next day, Walt went to his brother, Roy (who was in charge of the finances of the studio) and asked to spend $40 of the studio's money to buy a new suit. 'What do you need a suit for?' Roy asked. Walt replied, "Maybe I'll get married in it." Walt showed up in that brand-new suit a couple nights later and Lillian invited him in to meet her sister Hazel and her 7 year old niece, Marjorie.

Walt Disney took Lilly on a date to a movie one night in the spring of 1925. After the movie and a drive, he asked Lillian to marry him. Well, what he actually asked her was, "Lilly, this old car has seen better days (a Ford runabout). What do you think I should buy next, a new car or an engagement ring?" Lilly said a ring. A newly successful Walt bought both.

The Telegram & Mortimer Becomes Mickey

By 1928, Walt Disney and his studio had their first big hit character on their hands, Oswald the Lucky Rabbit. In the Spring of that year, 27-year-old Walt traveled (along with his wife, Lillian) from California to New York City to talk to Universal producer, Charles Mintz, about renegotiating his contract. Mintz wasn't interested. In fact, Mintz told Disney that he would have to take a pay cut of 20% per cartoon! He told Walt, "You know what? I've already hired every animator away from your studio except for Ub Iwerks. And you know your prize creation, Oswald? Well, I own him. You don't have the right to make any more Oswald pictures without me." At least that's how I'd like to think the dialogue went down; but the story is still the same. Mintz was right. Walt and Ub would need to finish their final three Oswald cartoons for Universal, then they'd be out of jobs.

Thankfully, Walt Disney was an eternal optimist. Before he and Lilly left New York City, Walt sent a telegram to his brother Roy who was back home in Los Angeles (pictured). If you can't read it, he had the telegrapher send: "LEAVING TONITE STOPPING OVER IN KC HOME SUNDAY MORNING SEVEN THIRTY DON'T WORRY EVERYTHING OK WILL GIVE DETAILS WHEN ARRIVE=WALT." I know it cost a penny per word in the 1920's (at least that's what I found when I researched), but there was no mention of failure or losing or anything in that message. As a matter of fact, when Roy picked up Walt and Lillian from the train station, Walt still didn't say anything. It wasn't until they got back to their homes on Lyric Avenue (Walt and Roy were next door neighbors back then) that Roy finally asked Walt, "Tell me about it kid—what kind of a deal did you make?" Walt told Roy the full story. He didn't let Roy get down about losing Oswald, though, telling him, "We're gonna make a new series!"

Walt Disney's iconic (and now in the public domain) Steamboat Willie.

It was then that Walt went to Ub Iwerks and explained the situation. Walt asked Ub to come up with several new characters, in secret, away from the other artists at the studio. According to a member of the Iwerks family who I've been in touch with, Ub came up with four: a cow (who later became Clarabelle), a frog (who later became Flip the Frog), a horse (who, down the line, was Horace Horsecollar) and, you guessed it, a mouse. Walt chose the mouse and, as legend has it, he wanted to call him Mortimer. It was Walt's wife, Lilly, who suggested Mickey.

Walt set Ub up in an office by himself, away from the other artists in the studio who were still completing the three remaining Oswald films. Ub would draw a few drawings of Oswald each day to use as a shield to cover the 700+ Mickey Mouse drawings he was pumping out each day for *Plane Crazy*. Walt then built a makeshift animation studio in his garage on Lyric Ave. Lilly, Edna Disney (Roy's wife), and others did the inking and painting on all of Ub's drawings. Walt himself would take them to the actual Walt Disney Studio, and he and a friend would do the recording. Each morning, when the rest of the studio employees would arrive, they would have no clue that Walt (and his new character Mickey Mouse) had been there just a couple of hours before.

Walt was able to finish *Plane Crazy* and had it previewed at a movie house on Sunset Boulevard. He paid the conductor of the orchestra a few bucks to play music over the gags in the film, and the audience responded to the gags and music in a way that encouraged Walt. He had seen one of the first "talkies," *The Jazz Singer*, and thought it was the future of film. The audience's reception of music and a short cartoon together in the theater that day inspired Walt to find a way to synchronize his cartoons to music and sound. His first animated film with synchronized sound, *Steamboat Willie*, was released just about six months later.

Walt's Nervous Breakdown

In the early 1930's, Walt and Lillian Disney's lives were very busy and stressful. Walt was the head of a flourishing Hollywood studio with the biggest cartoon star in the world, Mickey Mouse, headlining his cartoon shorts. His studio had grown from a storefront shop on Kingswell Avenue in Los Angeles to a bustling, busy animation studio in a brand new building that the Disney Brothers had built on Hyperion Avenue. Walt worked very late hours in those days, and he'd often not get home until well after the dinner Lillian had cooked for the two of them had gone cold. Walt and Lilly had been trying to conceive a child for years, and Lilly and suffered two miscarriages. The stress both at work and at home was really getting to the two of them, especially Walt.

Walt would take Lilly out to dinner some nights, then the two of them would stop by the studio; Walt would work on the latest cartoon or story and Lilly would fall asleep on the couch. Eventually, Walt started having trouble sleeping each night. He'd stare up at the ceiling, worrying about the problems of his work day and the bills he still had to pay. The stress started showing while he was at the studio as well. Walt started uncharacteristically snapping at his employees and losing his focus and concentration during story meetings. During one meeting with his animators, he became so frustrated that he began to cry.

The crying in front of his staff was a kind of rock bottom for Walt. He contacted his doctor, who asked him tons of questions about his work habits, home life, hobbies, etc. "You're having a nervous breakdown, Walt," the doctor said. "You've taken on too much and your mind can't handle it. You need to take a break and get total relaxation. Step away from the studio for a while. And now." He also recommended that Walt change his home routine when he returned from his vacation. The doctor encouraged Walt to start an exercise program and spend a little more time away from the studio. Walt decided that both the vacation and the new regimen seemed like a good idea, so he asked his brother, Roy, to run the studio while he was gone, and went home to tell Lilly to pack her bags!

The Disneys hadn't taken a vacation since their honeymoon six years before, so it was a welcome break from their crazy lives. Walt had always wanted to fulfill his childhood dream of riding a real paddlewheel riverboat down the Mississippi River like his boyhood idol Mark Twain, so he and Lillian headed to the St. Louis waterfront. Sadly, when they got there, they were told that the Great Depression had crushed the passenger riverboat business and the only boats headed down the "Mighty Mississipp" were barges. Undaunted, the Disneys took a train from St. Louis to Washington, D.C. to see the sights. They visited the Lincoln Memorial, the Capitol, Mount Vernon, and more. Then they boarded another train that took them down the East Coast of the U.S., all the way to Key West. They boarded a luxury cruise ship which took them to Havana, Cuba, where they spent a week, then boarded another cruise ship that took them through the Panama Canal and back up the coast of the Western United States where they eventually disembarked near Los Angeles. Walt and Lillian, after weeks away from the hustle and bustle of the city and the studio, couldn't have been more relaxed.

Walt returned to the studio shortly after returning home, but did not go back to his workaholic ways—at least not immediately! He listened to his doctor and started going to the Hollywood Athletic Club, where he enjoyed boxing, swimming, and running. He cut down on his work hours a bit and left work early on some days so that he and Lillian could go horseback riding in the hills behind their home. Lillian's doctor had encouraged her to pick up her physical activity as well. He thought that vigorous activity might help the couple conceive. Walt started golfing at the Griffith Park golf course on mornings before he'd go to the studio, often playing nine holes before work. Life was good, and Walt and Lillian were incredibly happy.

The vacation and exercise had paid off. Walt returned to the studio a new man and his immediate successes after his return proved it. *Flowers and Trees* and *The Three Little Pigs*, both Silly

Symphonies, were smash hits, with *Flowers and Trees* being awarded the first-ever award for a cartoon by the Academy of Motion Pictures. Even more importantly for the Disneys, Lilly gave birth to a healthy baby girl, Diane Marie, on December 18, 1933.

Walt Acts Out *Snow White* & Adriana Caselotti

Kansas City newspaper delivery boys were invited, in 1915, to view a silent, black-and-white version of *Snow White and the Seven Dwarfs*. Walt Disney was one of those kids in attendance. His memories of that performance would stay with him for the next 20+ years.

One night in the mid 1930s, Walt sent his animators to dinner at a restaurant across the street from the Disney Studio on Hyperion Avenue. When they returned, he was there to greet them. He asked them to accompany him to an empty soundstage that was lit by one bulb. They sat in chairs in a semicircle around their boss as Walt acted out each and every scene from *Snow White*. He played Snow White herself, all seven dwarfs, the Evil Queen, and the Prince. He acted and narrated for almost two hours, stirring potions with an evil gaze as the Queen and smiling with that famous twinkle in his eye as the dwarfs. When the performance was finally over there were actually grown men tearing up from Walt's stirring display. Walt looked at his core group of animators and said, 'This is going to be our first feature film.'

This story is in every Walt book, it seems. I first read it 20 years ago in Bob Thomas's biography, *Walt Disney: An American Original*. There's a part that doesn't really fit, but I love it and I wanted to add it on.

Adriana Caselotti was the voice actress who portrayed Snow White. When she originally made the movie, Walt and the Disney Company did not allow her to do any press or interviews about it. Snow White's voice was kept secret and Adriana was not able to perform the voice anywhere. Walt wanted to preserve the illusion that Snow White was a fairy tale. Adriana even sneaked into the premiere of the film and found a spot in the balcony to watch with the public. In 1944, though, the movie was re-released and she went on a full press tour with Pinto Colvig, the voices for Sleepy, Grumpy, and Dopey, among others.

In 1983 when Disneyland's Fantasyland got its makeover, a new Snow White recording of the song "I'm Wishing" was needed for Snow White's Wishing Well. Disney asked the then 67-year-old Adriana Caselotti if she'd reprise her role and she agreed, but on the day that she was recording, she just couldn't get it. Take after take went by, and, according to legend, she was down to her final attempt. She looked to the sky and said, "Walt, if you're out there, I need your help." She nailed the next take.

Walt Shows *Snow White* to Rosenberg

Midway through the production of 1937's *Snow White and the Seven Dwarfs*, Walt Disney was out of money. He asked his brother, Roy, to borrow more so that he could finish the film. Roy told Walt that he would need to show the work-in-progress *Snow White* to Bank of America executive Joseph Rosenberg, who was solely in charge of approving loans to movie studios. Walt said absolutely not. Roy insisted, telling Walt (something like) "If you want Joe to give you more money to finish this thing, you need to show him what he's paying for." Walt reluctantly agreed. He had workers at the studio work overtime to put the unfinished film together to show Joseph Rosenberg.

Rosenberg met Walt on a Saturday at the Disney Studio. He and Walt were the only two in the projection room as the film started. Only a few of the scenes were complete, with pencil sketches and blank sequences everywhere. Walt had to explain what was happening to Rosenberg throughout the screening, even filling in the dialogue in certain scenes. Rosenberg didn't say much during the screening. Walt watched him, waiting for huge reactions from everything that he was seeing, but those big reactions never came.

After the film ended, Walt walked Rosenberg to his car. They talked about all kinds of things that had nothing to do with the movie they had just watched. Walt was sweating as he watched the banker climb into his car and start the engine. "Thanks—goodbye!" he said. Then he added: "That thing is going to make a hatful of money.'"

Within Disney California Adventure is the Carthay Circle Restaurant. The building is a replica of the Carthay Circle Theater, a long-gone Hollywood theater where Snow White and the Seven Dwarfs premiered.

The Penthouse Club

After the success of *Snow White and the Seven Dwarfs*, Walt Disney was able to build his brand-new studio in Burbank. One of the features of the new studio was the Penthouse Club, located on the "roof" of the Animation Building, which was actually the fourth floor. Walt put his old childhood friend, Walt Pfieffer (in the left photo, on the left, next to Walt), in charge of running the members-only club, which featured a private restaurant, a barber shop, a bar, a gym with a personal trainer, and even steam baths. There were also card tables and pool tables for recreation, and even beds for guys who might've had too much to drink on their lunch hour.

Zoom in on the photo on the right and you can see that on the brochure for the Penthouse Club, it reads, "Penthouse Club: For all particulars, membership, and like that, check with Walt Pfeiffer. Men only! Sorry, gals..." and "Restaurant: 'Sa fact! We have the best equipped and most modern commissary in the Valley. Open to our personnel only at the following hours: 7:00 to 8:00 A.M., 11:30 to 1:30 at NOON, 5:00 to 6:00 P.M. (Tuesday and Thursday nights only)."

The problem with the Penthouse Club was that Walt accidentally created a class system at his studio. His intent with the club was to give the men that had been with him the longest, who had worked the hardest, a place to go and relax away from the rest of the studio. After originally only opening the club up to the artists and individuals who had been with the company the longest, he opened up membership to any man at the studio. The issue with this was, the monthly dues cost $9 or $10 per week, and the young artists at the studio could not afford that — the dues cost more than they made each week! This led to a bit of a divide between the old school artists and new artists at the Disney Studio, and this divide was one of the factors that went into the studio strike.

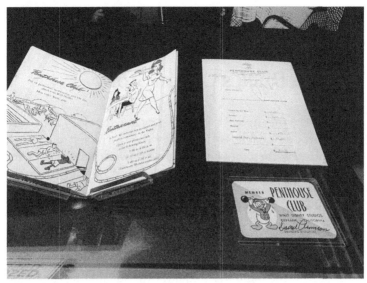

Check out the men sunbathing on the roof in the brochure.

Alright, I won't end this story on a bummer and tell you how the club eventually died out and went away. I'm going to end it this way: One of the stories the Imagineer Rolly Crump and other animators from that era used to tell was about the clothing optional sunbathing on the roof. Since it was a club full of guys only, they used to get a "full body tan" while on the roof and talking shop. St. Joseph's Hospital was right across the street, and apparently, once a brand-new, four story wing was added that was a little bit higher than the Disney Studio, the au-naturel activity had to stop! The nuns apparently had a pretty fantastic view!

Donald Duck's Origin Story

Late one evening in 1934, Walt Disney and his story men were sitting around a table, trying to get the the plot straightened out for a new cartoon short they were working on. At it for hours, they still couldn't figure it out. Walt told his guys, "That's it for tonight. Let's go get a good night's sleep and maybe we can figure it out in the morning."

Everyone started sauntering out of the room. One of the guys headed for a radio that was still playing a commercial and reached out to turn it off. 'Leave it on for a minute,' Walt said. The voice on the radio was a squawking, squabbling character. Walt laughed. "It's a duck!" he said. The story men that were left in the room all laughed and shook their heads. "Find out who does that voice! Maybe we can use him for a character!"

The actor on the radio who was doing the female duck voice turned out to be Clarence Nash, a voice actor who specialized in voices of barnyard animals. Walt invited him to the studio and as soon as he heard him perform his animal voices in person, he added Clarence to the talented pool of actors he already had working at the studio. He told Clarence, "I like that girl duck voice you do. We're going to find a way to use her in a cartoon!"

Months went by and there was another story meeting, this time about the Silly Symphony, *The Wise Little Hen*. A comedic character was needed to play opposite the hen. "What about that girl duck you've been wanting to use, Walt?" someone asked. Walt responded that he didn't think it would be funny to have two female characters squabbling. Then he had an idea. "That voice that Clarence does, it doesn't have to be a girl... it can be a boy duck...a good for nothing boy duck! We could really have some fun with that!" When one of the animators started sketching the rough outline of a duck character, Walt continued, "Make him kind of cocky. And give him something to wear. Ducks like the water. Put him in a sailor's costume!"

When the sketch looked the way Walt wanted, Donald Duck was added to the expanding list of recurring Disney animated characters. His first appearance was, in fact, in *The Wise Little Hen* and his first line ever spoken was "Who...me? Oh no! I got a bellyache!" when the hen asked him for help. Donald's second performance was opposite Disney's biggest star, Mickey Mouse, in *The Orphan's Benefit*.

The Carolwood Pacific Railroad

In the spring of 1948, Walt Disney was a very busy man. The Disney Studio Nurse, Hazel George, suggested that he take some time off to visit the Chicago Railroad Fair. Being an enormous train buff, Walt agreed to take the trip. He knew his wife, Lillian, and his daughters would not be interested, so he asked his friend and colleague, fellow railroad enthusiast Ward Kimball, to join him on the train ride out to Chicago for the fair.

Walt and Ward had a fantastic time. So fantastic, as a matter of fact, that Walt came home to Los Angeles and told Lilly, "That was the most fun I've ever had! I'm building a backyard railroad!" Walt and Lillian started looking for a new home as a 25th anniversary present to themselves. Walt really had no interest in a new home, he just wanted enough room for his

Walt Disney's actual backyard railroad engine, the Lilly Belle, on display at the Walt Disney Family Museum.

railroad. They settled on the perfect plot of land on Carolwood Drive in the Holmby Hills section of Los Angeles, and architects got busy designing the home, while folks at the Disney Studio began designing the railroad, complete with bridges, overpasses, and miles of railroad track!

When construction finally began on both, there was a problem. Lilly believed Walt's railroad would be contained on one side of the backyard while Walt believed he had free reign to build the railroad across the entire yard. Lilly told Walt that she had had plans for the big hill in the yard, and that it was to become home to her new flowerbeds.

Walt had to think. They property was already purchased and construction had started. How as he going to get his train AND make sure Lillian also got her flowers? It came to him one day on the way to the Studio. He went in one morning and had the studio attorneys write up a "legal contract" that would permit Walt to build a railroad tunnel UNDER Lilly's flowerbeds. Both Lilly and Walt signed off on the contract, and construction of the railroad tunnel began.

Once construction of the tunnel was underway, Walt stopped by one day to see the progress. One of the architects showed Walt the plan for the tunnel, and explained to Walt that the tunnel wouldn't get very dark. With an opening at each end and no turns throughout the tunnel, the sunlight would shine right through. That drove Walt crazy. He redrew the design of the tunnel under the flowerbeds, making it an S-curve so that his riders were left in total darkness for a moment. When the architect saw it, he told Walt, "Mr. Disney, this is going to cost way more money if we do it your way." Walt responded, "If I was worried about what it cost, I wouldn't do it at all! We are going to do it right."

Daddy's Day

I've wanted to share a bit about Diane Disney Miller, Walt and Lillian's older daughter. Lillian had experienced a couple of miscarriages before Diane's birth, and then had another one after. The doctors advised her not to try to have any more children. Walt and Lillian were sad, of course, but soon adopted a second daughter, who they named Sharon Mae Disney.

Walt really loved being a dad and a husband. You can find videos of him playing with his daughters in the backyard and throwing them in the air in the family's new swimming pool at their home on Woking Way in Los Angeles. You've probably heard or read this elsewhere, but Saturday was "Daddy's Day" in the Disney household, and Walt would take both of his daughters out for the day each Saturday, on his day off. The trio would end up at the Griffith Park Carousel on most Saturdays. Walt would eat peanuts while Sharon and Diane rode the carousel horses. Often Walt would take Diane and Sharon to the Disney Studio in Burbank, where the entire studio lot became their playground. Both girls learned to ride their bikes on the studio lot. (In later years, Walt would bring Diane's son, Christopher, to the studio where he would let his grandson tour around the sound stages in a Disneyland Autopia car; don't grandparents always spoil their grandkids?!)

He drove both of his daughters to school every single day that he could up until both of them had their driver's licenses. Not only did Walt drive Diane and Sharon, but he'd normally have a whole gang of tweens and teens in his car (Diane and Sharon's friends), and he'd drop them all off each morning. Diane had said that she thought her dad got a lot of the ideas for "The Parent Trap" from the family stories he listened to while driving all of those girls to school every day!

What really came from those Daddy's Days, though, was the idea for a brand new, family experience. A place where parents and their children could have fun together. In a 1963 interview, Walt revealed a bit more on the inspiration for The Happiest Place on Earth.

"Well, it [Disneyland] came about when my daughters were very young and I...Saturday...was always Daddy's day with the two daughters. So we'd start out and try to go someplace, you know, different things, and I'd take them to the merry-go-round and I took them different places and as I'd sit while they rode the merry-go-round and did all these things... sit on a bench, you know, eating peanuts....I felt that there should be something built...some kind of amusement enterprise built...where the parents and the children could have fun together. So that's how Disneyland started. Well, it took many years...it was a...oh, a period of maybe 15 years developing. I started with many ideas, threw them away, started all over again. And eventually, it evolved into what you see today at Disneyland. But it all started from a daddy with two daughters wondering where he could take them where he could have a little fun with them too."

This bench, from the Walt Disney Family Museum, is one of the original benches that Walt sat on at Griffith Park while watching his daughters ride the carousel.

Walt & Herb Ryman's Lost Weekend

It was Saturday morning, September 26, 1953. Disney artist Herb Ryman, who was not working for Disney at the time, was painting in his home when he got a call from Dick Irvine, a former colleague, who told him he was at the Disney Studio with Walt Disney. Walt asked Dick to put Herb on the phone.

Walt: How soon can you get here to the studio, Herbie?

Herb: It's Saturday! What are you doing at the studio on a Saturday?

Walt: It's my studio! I'll be here on a Saturday whenever I want! Listen, how soon can you get here?

Herb: In about 15 minutes if I come as I am or 30 minutes if I take a shower.

Walt: Come as you are! Herbie, we're gonna build an amusement park!

Herb: Great, Walt! Where are you going to build it?

Walt: We were going to build it across the street from the studio, but it's much too big for that now! We're looking for a place.

Herb: What are you going to call it?

Walt: Disneyland.

Herb: Well, that's a good a name as any!

Walt: Herbie, look, my brother is going to New York City to talk to the bankers. They won't just give us the money for this thing, we need to show them what we are going to build.

Herb: That's great, Walt! I'd love to see the drawing! Where can I see it?

Walt: You're going to draw it!

Herb: No, I'm not! This is the first I've ever heard of this. I'm not going to do it. I'm going to embarrass myself and you! I won't make a fool of the two of us!

Walt assured Herb that he knew he could do it. Herb could hear the emotion in Walt's voice as he told him, "Herbie, this is my dream. I've wanted this for years and I need your help. You're the only one who can do it. I'll stay here with you and we'll do it together."

Herb was there in 15 minutes. Walt explained in extraordinary detail what he wanted the park to look like. For 42 straight hours, Walt Disney talked and Herb Ryman drew. They had food delivered and kept the coffee flowing. When Dick Irvine and Marvin Davis showed up for work on Monday morning, the room was trashed, and Walt and Herb were still there, exhausted, but finished. The result was the original Disneyland drawing that Roy O. Disney took to New York City that following week.

This is one of those stories that you can find in lots of different places. The direct quote is from *Walt Disney's Railroad Story* by historian Michael Broggie. And here's one from Leslie Iwerks' book, *The Imagineering Story*: "Ryman had only one demand: a big chocolate malted milkshake. He got it."

Hiding Iwao

One thing I've learned over the years of researching the early days of the Disney Company and speaking to Disney notables like Floyd Norman and the late Rolly Crump is that the Disney animators loved gags. They played practical jokes on one another constantly, and it seems like the only one who was off limits for a joke was Walt Disney himself. Walt wasn't a grump, he'd laugh at the appropriate things, but when he was at work, he was working. He didn't have time for jokes or silly distractions. He did understand that his employees needed those distractions, though, so he took the craziness in stride.

My favorite gag story was one I've heard Imagineer Rolly Crump tell. Rolly was originally hired as an "in-betweener" and eventually was recruited by Walt himself to move over to WED (later renamed Walt Disney Imagineering) after Walt had noticed some spinning propellers that Rolly had designed. This gag involves two other famous names: Imagineer Ward Kimball and Disney and Hanna Barbera animator Iwao Takamoto. Iwao was hired by the Disney Studio in 1945 and was an animator and character designer for *Cinderella*, *Peter Pan*, *Sleeping Beauty*, and *One Hundred and One Dalmatians*. For Hanna Barbera, Iwao came up with the original designs for Scooby Doo and Astro from the Jetsons, among others.

So Ward Kimball was Iwao Takamato's boss at the Disney Studio. In the 1940s and 50s, the studio was a bustling place and tours came through almost daily. The animators always loved coming up with gags to confuse the poor guests on the tour! Rolly said that against the wall in the office where Ward, Iwao, and other animators worked was a small closet or cabinet. For this one gag, Iwao went into the tiny closet (clearly barely big enough for one person to fit inside) when they heard the tour coming down the hall. While Ward was talking to the tour group, explaining the new film they were working on an how the animation process worked, a knock came from inside the closet!

"Yes, who is it?" Ward asked? "It's Iwao!" a voice from inside the tiny closet said. "Okay, I'll be right there," Ward said as he walked across the room while not breaking character and still talking to the group. He asked them to excuse him for a moment while he answered "the door."

Ward opened the closet door and out jumped Iwao Takamoto, work-in-progress cartoon scene in his hand. "Ward, can you please take a look at this scene for me?" Ward took the paper from Iwao and studied it for a moment to the astonishment of the group of confused guests. Ward said something like, "Not bad. Make this eyebrow stand out a little more and darken this line and it'll work." Iwao thanked him for his time, turned, walked back into the tiny closet and closed the door behind him. Rolly said that the best part of the whole gag was that the tour group stayed inside Ward's office for another fifteen minutes and poor Iwao had to stay in there to make the joke work! Can you imagine just how confused those poor people must've been?! That thought absolutely kills me!

Walt and the Wienies of Disneyland

When it came to what he ate, Walt Disney was a simple guy. His favorites were basic foods like fried chicken (I think that is what he's eating in the photo), chili (he was a canned chili connoisseur, often mixing two of his favorite brands together), sandwiches, and hot dogs, or as Walt called them, "wienies." Of course, this was long before the term "wienie" or "weenie" became something for my kids to laugh at (fine, me too). It was simply short for wienerwurst, the name German immigrants gave to what we now call hot dogs. Walt grew up calling hot dogs that, and it just stuck throughout his entire life.

When Disneyland was in the earliest stages, Walt and his family had a standard poodle who Walt named Duchess Disney, or DeeDee for short. He would take the dog everywhere he went, even to the Disney Studio, and she was much more HIS dog than the rest of the family's. When Walt would come home from the

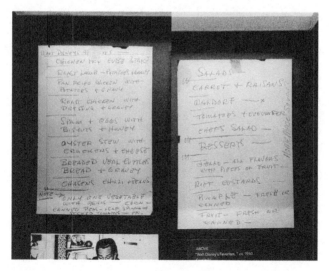

Walt's handwritten notes to his cook and housekeeper, Thelma Howard.

studio he would park his car in the family garage and enter the house through the kitchen, stopping at the fridge to grab some "wienies" to share with Dee Dee.

According to the late Jim Korkis and his chat with Walt's daughter Diane Disney Miller in his book *The Vault of Walt Volume 5*: "He would go to the refrigerator and pull out two uncooked hot dogs, one for himself and one for the dog. He would play with her, wiggling the hot dog around, and she would go wherever he moved around and was so happy when she finally got her treat. It was part of an evening ritual and both of them loved it and looked forward to it."

It was in those precious moments with DeeDee that Walt had the idea for the "wienies" of Disneyland. Attractions like Sleeping Beauty Castle, the *Mark Twain* Riverboat, and more are visual icons in the distance when you enter Disneyland, beckoning you to come in and explore further, just like Walt did when he enticed DeeDee to follow him around for that treat. When Walt explained that to his theme park designers, they figured out exactly what he was hoping for!

I feel compelled to include a "cute" and related story about Imagineer Rolly Crump here. When he was in Tokyo working on Tokyo Disneyland, he was explaining how Walt would use wienies to draw in guests to a room full of Japanese designers. He went on and on about them, saying wienie-this and wienie-that. The Japanese people are so polite. He finished his talk and asked if there were any questions. A female designer raised her hand and said, "Mr. Crump? What is a wienie?" Rolly said he'd use the word carrot after that!

Town Square Flagpole

It was April of 1955, and Disneyland was a hotbed of construction and activity. Walt Disney was sitting on some steps near the Disneyland Firehouse, joined by his friend, set designer and decorator Emile Kuri. The two were enjoying their brown bag lunches, looking over Town Square, when a thought occurred to Walt. "Emile, what are you gonna do for a (Town Square) flagpole?" Emile showed Walt the sketch that he had been working on of a flagpole cast in bronze. Walt took a look at the sketch and liked what he saw, but tole Emile that money was incredibly tight, and unless things were cut, there wouldn't be enough money to finish the park by Opening Day. "Just put up an aluminum pole," Walt told him.

That evening, Emile was driving down Wilshire Boulevard in Los Angeles, on his way to a Board of Governors meeting, when he came upon an accident where a truck had hit an old street lamp and knocked it down. It was a beautiful, antique lamp with an ornate base. Emile pulled over and asked the L.A. city worker in charge what would happen to the base. Scrap iron was the answer.

From John Kuri: "Dad contacted L.A. City Public Works the next day, purchased the undamaged base for 5-cents a pound, had it fitted with a sleeve to the aluminum flagpole, sent it to the park and had it installed. When Walt saw it he turned to my Dad and said, 'Emile, I told you not to spend the money.' Dad explained. Walt threw his arms around my Dad and said, 'That's why I love you!' Dad acquired lampposts from Baltimore, Maryland, San Jose, Philadelphia, all on trips he took with Walt and Lilly shopping for the the elements that make the original Disneyland so authentic."

Sleeping Beauty Castle

If you've seen any of those old sketches, some black and white and some with light coloring on them, those are probably sketches from Imagineer Herb Ryman. Herb was the guy who Walt Disney spent the weekend with in 1953 where Walt told him all about what he wanted his park to look like, and then Herb sketched it all out for him. So, the giant map that you have probably seen, the original drawing and map of Disneyland, that is the one that Herb drew and that Walt's brother Roy O. Disney took to the bankers in New York to try to sell the idea of Disneyland.

Once Disneyland was given the green light, Walt chose his old pal Herb Ryman to design Sleeping Beauty Castle. As a matter of fact, the castle didn't have a name at that point. When Herb was dreaming it up, it was called "Fantasyland Castle," and it wasn't until much later on that it got the name "Sleeping Beauty Castle." Now, Herb Ryman was a guy who had traveled quite a bit, and he had actually visited "The Mad King" Ludwig's castle in Bavaria, Castle Neuschwanstein. So, Herb had that castle in mind when he designed Sleeping Beauty Castle, and model makers at WED had first designed a solid, one piece scale model, and then later built a more detailed, movable scale model.

Herb Ryman and his fellow Imagineers had shown up on time for a meeting with Walt Disney where Walt would "check their work." The model of Sleeping Beauty Castle was built in pieces, then put together. Herb was fiddling around with the model when he turned the front, top section of the castle 180 degrees and made it face the opposite direction. Someone in the meeting told Herb to stop messing around and that Walt would be entering the room at any second. At the moment where Herb reached to switch the top oft he castle back, reverting to the original design, Walt walked into the room. He took a look at it and said something along the lines of,

"That's better. That'll work!" And that is the story of how the original back of Sleeping Beauty Castle got switched around and made into the front! If you look at the photo I've attached, you can see that the top of the castle is actually the side that faces Fantasyland today, not the Hub!

A look at an original Sleeping Beauty Castle model from the Walt Disney Family Museum. A sharp eye can see that the front of the model actually ended up at the rear of the castle!

Harriet Burns

Harriet Burns began working at the Disney Studio in 1955 as a set designer and painter on the show, the Mickey Mouse Club. Known as "The First Lady of Walt Disney Imagineering," Harriet was one of the three original employees of WED (later renamed Walt Disney Imagineering, or WDI), along with Fred Joerger and Wathel Rogers. They were a part of the now-famous Disney machine shop, but actually worked out of a small boxcar near the machine shop. Having only three individuals working there in the early days allowed Harriet to develop a very close working relationship with Walt Disney.

Harriet, Fred, and Wathel's work area at the studio became known as the WED Model Shop. Within that shop, Harriet created the original scale models for now iconic Disneyland attractions like Sleeping Beauty Castle, the Matterhorn, Pirates of the Caribbean, and more. Outside of the Model Shop, she designed and painted the sets for Disneyland's Submarine Voyage and worked on sets and character designs for the Haunted Mansion and Great Moments with Mr. Lincoln and the Carousel of Progress at the New York World's Fair.

One of Harriet's most endearing and enduring designs in Disneyland, and the one that you've probably noticed in person, is the feathers on the birds in the Tiki Room, in particular their chest plumage. She was having the hardest time trying to figure out how to make the birds look like they were breathing throughout the show. Nothing she tried worked. One day, Walt paid her a visit at the Model Shop. He was wearing a blue, wool sweater (the same one you've seen in the old *Disneyland* TV shows). Apparently Walt moved his arms an awful lot when he talked, he was a very animated talker, and Harriet noticed that the fabric of the sweater by his elbows would expand and contract in just the way she was looking for when he bent his elbows. It was a light bulb moment, and all of the tiki birds have had that same type of fabric on their chest plates ever since!

Tempus Fugit

On July 13, 1955, at "six o'clock in the afternoon," or so it said on the invitation to Walt & Lillian Disney's "Tempus Fugit Celebration," the couple invited 300 of their closest friends to Disneyland just four days before it opened to celebrate their 30th wedding anniversary!

Admiral Joe Fowler was impatiently waiting for the horse drawn carriages to arrive at the *Mark Twain*'s dock in Frontierland. He had walked from the big, wooden Frontierland entrance gate at the Hub to the dock, just a few minutes before 6:00, and he saw a woman in a dress frantically sweeping the deck of the ship. As he got closer, he saw it was actually Lillian Disney. She told him to grab a broom, as the Mark Twain was filthy with construction debris and was not ready for guests. Admiral Fowler and Lilly finished cleaning the deck just as the first guests started making their way down the beautifully lit, brand new Main Street USA.

Once all guests were on board, the Mark Twain's whistle gave a warning, and the ship made its "Maiden Voyage" around the Rivers of America with Walt, Lillian, and all of their closest friends and family. A jazz band played New Orleans style music as the ship made its way around Tom Sawyer Island. Waiters walked around the ship, handing out mint juleps (with alcohol) to guests. Walt himself had a couple of drinks, and then a couple more during dinner and the show that followed at the Golden Horseshoe.

Toward the end of the show, there was an entire finale where Pecos Bill would shoot off his "guns" in the theater. All of a sudden, someone pointed to the balcony, and there was Walt, pointing his finger guns back at Pecos Bill! He then decided he wanted to be on the stage, so Walt apparently hung off the balcony and lowered himself down, making it to the stage without injuring himself. He was exhausted from the months he had put in to make his dream happen, and he just stood there, beaming, smiling at the crowd. The crowd started chanting, "Speech! Speech!" thinking it was a good opportunity for him to say something, but Walt didn't. He just smiled. After the party was over, Walt's family did not want him driving home. Whether it was the mint juleps or just pure exhaustion and adrenaline, they didn't think it was a good idea. Walt was a proud guy and they totally expected him to fire back at them but he didn't. His daughter, Diane, said he actually got in the back of his car, rolled up some Disneyland blueprints, and starting singing into her ear and playing it like a trumpet. After a few minutes, her dad was quiet. She looked in the backseat and there was Walt Disney, asleep, with his blueprint trumpet still in his folded arms!

The Night Before Disneyland

It was the evening of July 16, 1955, the night before Disneyland's Grand Opening that was to be aired on live television. Walt was spending his night in the 20,000 Leagues Under the Sea walkthrough exhibit with Ken Anderson. Ken was trying to get the mechanical arms of the squid to work and Walt was there, spray gun in hand, painting the wall of the backdrop behind the giant monster black. Eventually, when the arms wouldn't work and the paint wasn't done, Walt and Ken called it a night. The 20,000 Leagues attraction would have to open a few days late.

Walt and Ken walked out to Town Square where they sat on a curb to get some fresh air and take a little break. As they were sitting there, resting for probably the first time that day, an electrician came running out of Fantasyland. "Mr. Disney, there's no power to the Toad ride! Someone cut the power lines!" Ken told Walt that he'd go take care of it so Walt could get some rest. When Ken made his way to Mr. Toad's Wild Ride, he discovered that the cables weren't cut, they were just unplugged. Once Ken got Mr. Toad's Wild Ride up and running again, he took a seat backstage behind the attraction to get some rest himself. As the story goes, Ken Anderson fell asleep and missed almost all of Disneyland's Opening Day!

Walt himself took a final lap of Main Street USA, making sure that everything looked good for the opening. He then climbed the staircase to his apartment over the firehouse, climbed into bed, and tried to get some sleep. For the next two hours, the phone rang off the hook with workers and media and last minute requests for the next day's festivities. Eventually, Walt took the phone off the hook to get a few hours sleep.

This is a story I've heard before from Bob Gurr and others, but this specific one comes from Jim Denny's book, *Walt's Disneyland*. I wanted to share a quote from that book, too, because it ties up this story really nicely!

When Disneyland's gates opened the next morning, Walt watched the people stream into the park from that famous window in his apartment above the firehouse. He was joined by the Mouseketeers from the Mickey Mouse Club. Mouseketeer Sharon Baird later recalled:

"I was standing next to him at the window, watching the guests come pouring through the gates. When I looked up at him, he had his hands behind his back, a grin from ear to ear. I could see a lump in his throat and a tear streaming down his cheek. He had realized his dream. I was only twelve years old at the time, so it didn't mean as much to me then. But as the years go by, that image of him becomes more and more endearing."

The author and his family in Walt Disney's privte Disneyland apartment.

Bob Gurr's Memories of Opening Day

It was the morning of July 17, 1955. Disneyland's big Opening Day event, in a matter of hours, would be airing live on television. My friend Bob Gurr arrived to his parking spot close to 9am. When he arrived at the lineup for the Opening Day procession down Walt Disney's brand spanking new Main Street USA, Walt was already milling about. There were nine Autopia cars sitting outside the Opera House, ready to go, and Bob knew one of his many jobs for the day was making sure they all made it down Main Street for the television cameras. Walt approached Bob with 50's TV Star Gale Storm and her two sons who Bob guessed were around 7 or 8 years old.

After introducing everyone all around, Walt looked at Ms. Storm and said, "Well, there are lots of other things I want to show you around the park. Bobby here is going to take care of your boys for the day." Of course, Bob did as he was told. You didn't

The author and Bob Gurr.

question Walt Disney, especially not on the day his dream was about to come true!

Bob drove one of Gale's sons in an Autopia car down Main Street on live TV, while her other son was driven in another car with another driver that was probably given the task by Walt himself. A little later Bob found himself in the same car on the Autopia track, chasing down other Autopia cars. When Gale's son asked Bob to bump the car in front of him, he obliged. The angry driver, an African American gentleman in glasses, turned to tell Bob to take it easy. The driver of the other car was Sammy Davis Jr.

Bob didn't ditch the kiddos until it was almost dark that night. Most of his day was spent on the Autopia track, kickstarting stalled cars. As he told D23, "After Disneyland opened, we had a lot of trouble with the Autopia cars. The majority of them were failing, and no one had figured out the support side of the attractions. I had been with my own tools, repairing the cars on-site. Walt came by, looked at the whole scene and asked, 'What do you need?' I told him we needed mechanics to work on the cars, and we didn't have any kind of facilities. In less than an hour, here comes this tractor dragging an old building and the driver says, 'Here's your damn building. Walt told me to bring it to you. Where do you want it?' We had mechanics the next morning."

Cornelius Vanderbilt Wood

Cornelius Vanderbilt Wood, who went by C.V., was hired by the Stanford Research Institute in the early 1950's where he worked as an engineer and as an outside consultant to Walt Disney, helping with the logistics of the construction of Disneyland. Walt was so impressed by Wood's intelligence and problem-solving capabilities that he offered him a job as the supervisor of the construction of Disneyland.

Walt and Woody (Walt's nickname for Wood) were both fiery, passionate individuals and became close very quickly. Walt trusted Woody and named him Disneyland's very first employee. Wood not only supervised the construction of the park, he actually assisted Harrison "Buzz" Price, who chose the site among the orange groves of Anaheim AND was in charge of purchasing the land where the park was built.

It was C.V. Wood who, as Vice President and General Manager of Disneyland, gave Vice President Nixon the Key To Disneyland in August of 1955, one month after the grand opening of the park. If you're anything like I was and you've never heard of this guy before, this doesn't make any sense, right? How could a man who was so deeply involved with the construction and creation of Disneyland, a man who Walt Disney often referred to as "a son," be totally left out of all of the Disney history books and films? Why doesn't Cornelius Vanderbilt Wood have a window on Main Street U.S.A. in Disneyland, the park that he was so incredibly instrumental in making a reality?

The answer is a bit of a complicated one. In July of 1956, just one year after the opening of Disneyland, C.V. Wood was gone. Not only was he out as Disneyland's Vice President and General Manager, he was wiped clean from all of the historical accounts of the Disney company as well. Walt Disney had his older brother, Roy O. Disney (another key figure in the history of the Disney company, but that story is for another post!) fire

Wood reportedly after a heated argument. It's not known what that argument was about and neither Walt Disney nor his brother Roy ever went public with the true reason why Wood was fired so abruptly.

There were rumors that Wood had embezzled money from the Disneys and their company, but there were never any legal proceedings or records that would prove that as a fact. Other speculated reasons for the firing were that Wood was taking too much credit publicly for the creation of Disneyland or that he was fired because he was designing other theme parks behind Walt Disney's back. Whatever the reason, Wood's relationship with the Disney Company ended swiftly and without much fanfare. It was like one day, C.V. Wood was in the Disneyland offices, holding meetings like he always did, and the next day he was gone and never spoken of again.

When his new theme park Freedomland U.S.A. opened in the Bronx in 1960, it seemed like Wood was finally going to achieve the fame and fortune that Walt Disney had achieved with Disneyland's opening in 1955. The park was made up of several themed lands including Little Old New York, Chicago (which had daily shows depicting the Chicago Fire of 1871), The Great Plains, San Fransisco, The Old Southwest, New Orleans Mardi Gras, and Satellite City: The Future. If any of these ideas sound familiar at all, they should! They were designed an awful lot like Disneyland's themed lands as Wood was trying to create an east coast version of the popular west coast tourist destination. On the day that Freedomland U.S.A. opened, The Ed Sullivan Show hosted a preview of the new theme park, calling it Disneyland's equal on the east coast. The following day, traffic was backed up so badly in the Bronx with cars trying to get to the park that Freedomland U.S.A. had to stop selling park tickets.

The initial success of the "East Coast Disneyland" was very short-lived, however, and by the end of it's first year of operation, Freedomland U.S.A. was already over $8 million in debt. After a few more struggling years, the park was met with the extremely tough competition of the 1964 New York World's Fair (Walt Disney's ultimate retribution on his old pal Woody) and Freedomland U.S.A. filed for bankruptcy and was later torn down. On the site in the Bronx where the park once stood now stands Co-Op City, a large residential development, and the Bay Plaza Shopping Center. A plaque was installed in 2013 commemorating the theme park that once stood on that location.

After his most ambitious theme park was shut down, C.V. Wood did achieve some fame and fortune when he moved the London Bridge from London to Arizona and opened it up as a tourist attraction. He then was hired by Warner Brothers where he worked until his death in 1992. The Disney Company still does not acknowledge any link to Wood to this day, and his existence is still completely wiped out of the "official" history of Disneyland and the Disney Company. It's doubtful that anyone will ever know the true reason why Wood and Walt Disney had the intense falling out that they had as almost everyone who knew either man isn't around to tell their stories any longer. Just remember, the next time you're in Disneyland or Walt Disney World, that yes, Walt Disney was in fact a genius and a visionary. Disneyland was his dream project, his creation, and one of his greatest accomplishments. But also remember, Walt Disney had a little bit of help in realizing his dream, and that help's name was Cornelius Vanderbilt Wood.

Feral Cats in the Castle

It was July 17, 1955, the giant Opening Day press and television event for Disneyland. On that chaotic day, Van France was walking backstage when he spotted C.V. Wood, the General Manager of Disneyland. C.V. yelled at Van, "We forgot to lock the doors to Sleeping Beauty Castle! There are guests inside! Get them out of there!" On Opening Day, the interior of the castle was nothing more than wooden planks, stairs, and ladders. Not a safe place for a guest to be!

Of course, nothing that happened on Opening Day escaped Walt Disney. When he found out about the guests and their interest in what was going on inside the castle, he decided to act on it. During a busy day in the park, Walt asked Imagineer Ken Anderson and set designer/decorator Emile Kuri to join him for a stroll inside Sleeping Beauty Castle. According to Ken, the castle was inhabited at the time by close to one hundred feral cats!

Walt, the one-time farm boy from Marceline, MO, apparently just walked around the cats as if they weren't even there. He told Ken, "There's not a lot of room in here, but we need something for the guests to walk through and see. I know you can do it!" As Walt was showing Ken around the small space, Emile was off to the side on his own. Oh, Ken mentioned in this story that Emile was wearing a beautiful, all white suit. Emile picked up a bag from the ground that a bunch of the cats had been sleeping in. All of a sudden, Ken realized that Emile's suite was gray! Emile started jumping around, slapping at his arms and legs! Ken looked at himself, then Walt. Their clothes were turning gray, too! They were covered in THOUSANDS of fleas!

Walt grabbed a phone from the wall and made a call. Apparently the person on the other line didn't catch what he said because of the hysteria and screaming of his words. 'Walt who?!' he yelled into the receiver when the answerer didn't recognize his voice. "Walt Disney! Send us a car to get us out of here!"

Within minutes, a motorcycle with a sidecar showed up outside the castle. A sidecar. Only one seat. Walt looked at Ken and Emile and said, "I'll send another car for you. Whatever you do, don't go out through the crowd!" A few minutes passed. Ken and Emile took off through the crowd, running as fast as they could to wardrobe so they could change and shower.

When they finished at wardrobe, Walt was outside, laughing. "You didn't go through the crowd, did you guys?!" They assured him that they had not. "Then, how the hell did you get here so fast?!"

Walt ended up having all of those cats gathered up, bathed, groomed, and relocated to new homes. Ken Anderson designed a walkthrough diorama of Sleeping Beauty scenes that remained in Sleeping Beauty Castle until 1977. New walkthroughs and scenes have replaced it over the years, but you can still currently walk through the castle, just as Walt wanted.

Sleeping Beauty Castle in Disneyland.

Walt Meets the Nuns

Rolly Crump told me a story that he told many times on other podcasts and Disney documentaries. One afternoon, Emile Kuri and Walt were sitting on a bench (or maybe a curb; the story changed a bit between tellings, as legends often do) and eating peanuts. He noticed a nun walking through the park holding a rope in her hands. Walking behind the nun were seven or eight young children, all with that rope tied around their waists. Holding the other end of the rope was another nun.

Walt was intrigued. He jogged over to ask the nun in front what was going on. She explained to Walt that the nuns were a part of an orphanage. They had saved just enough money to bring the children to Disneyland and ride a few rides. Walt told the nuns to wait right where they stood. He ran off to the Main Entrance of the park, got the money back that the nuns had paid for themselves and the kids, and grabbed them handfuls of free ticket books. When he got back to the nuns and the orphans, he handed them everything, explained to them that no kids in need would ever have to pay to get into his park, and he set them up with a free lunch a little later at the Red Wagon Inn. Walt took his place again next to Emile, who was still eating peanuts on that bench (or curb, or maybe it was the steps of City Hall), and said, "That was fun!"

Tom Nabbe Becomes Tom Sawyer

Tom Nabbe lived about 3/4 of a mile from Disneyland's construction site and the eventual Happiest Place on Earth. He and his buddies would ride their bikes to an overpass on Harbor Boulevard to watch as the park changed from bulldozers and building frames to Main Street, U.S.A. and Sleeping Beauty Castle. He was outside the park for the Press Opening on July 17, 1955, with his mom who was looking for celebrities. When she spotted actor Danny Thomas and asked him for an autograph, he leaned in and whispered, asking if she'd been inside the park as he signed her book. When Tom's mother said no, he told her, 'I've got a couple of extra tickets for you and your son.' Tom and his mom got to enjoy the park on its most infamous day. He said that it was the trashiest he'd ever seen a Disney park and that image surely stuck with Walt Disney for the rest of his days. Cleanliness became a top priority.

Tom wasn't deterred, though! He returned the next day with a friend, paying the admission to get in. He told me that was the only day in his entire life that he paid to get into a Disney theme park. The next day, on July 19, 1955, 12 year old Tom began his career as a Disneyland news boy. If he sold 100 newspapers outside the park, the owners of the Disneyland News stand would allow him to come inside the gates of the park to sell more papers to the Disneyland guests. This went on for a few months, and then Tom caught word that Walt Disney himself was constructing a Tom Sawyer Island right in the middle of Frontierland. Other newsies and Disneyland workers encouraged Tom to approach Walt about playing Tom Sawyer on the island. He looked the part and was used to the limelight a little bit already, since his photo was often used for promotions for the newstand in 1955. From Tom:

"Somebody told me that Walt was going to build Tom Sawyer Island...and you look just like Tom Sawyer and you should ask him for a job. And I thought that was one heck of an idea. And Walt was in the park quite frequently; as you know he had the apartment above the fire station. So he'd drive down on a Friday afternoon and then spend Friday and Saturday (in the park) and then he'd stop at the studio on Sundays. So he'd be out in the park and wandering around and pretty much talking to folks until he'd get inundated with too many people wanting his autograph, then he'd move off backstage for a while. But I found him and introduced myself and told him I'd heard he was building Tom Sawyer's Island and that I looked just like Tom Sawyer and he should hire me! Uhhh...well, he didn't. But he didn't say no. He said he'd think about it. So he left the door open.

"So, through the next seven, eight months, any time I'd find Walt, I'd ask him, 'Are you still thinking about hiring me to play Tom Sawyer?!' And I remember one conversation we had, he told me, 'I could put a dummy or a mannequin over there and it wouldn't be leaving every five minutes for a hot dog and a Coke!' Then I think it was late may of '56, I had finished up selling my newspapers and I was in the Penny Arcade playing the baseball machine and a gentleman by the name of Dick Nunis came up and tapped me on the shoulder. Dick was the supervisor of Frontierland and he said, 'Tom, come with me.' I don't know if that name means anything to you, but when Dick says come with me, you don't argue with Dick, you go with Dick.

"So we went over to Frontierland and Walt and Morgan "Bill" Evans, the landscape architect for Disneyland and actually for Walt's house and Walt Disney World, they were coming off the island on a raft, and Walt said, 'Well, you still wanna be Tom Sawyer?' I told him, 'Absolutely Mr. Disney, I do!' Now, understand that Walt worked with a lot of kids around this time frame. He had the Mickey Mouse Club, and child actors, and he was very comfortable to talk with. He'd listen to what you had to say. He pretty much told me, 'You need to get a work permit and a social security card and once you do that, we'll put you on as Tom Sawyer.'"

Tom went on to portray Tom Sawyer on nights, weekends, and holidays throughout junior high and high school. His career with the Disney Company spanned almost 50 years and he

was the last working member of Club 55, a group of original
Disneyland cast members named for Disneyland's inaugural
year and for their chief qualification of membership—a pay-
check from Walt Disney dated 1955.

Timing the Jungle Cruise

For the first seven years of Disneyland, the Jungle Cruise was Adventureland's only attraction. Walt had originally wanted live animals to inhabit the banks along the Jungle Rivers of the World (the attraction's original name) but, when he realized that guests would not get a "consistent, good show" with live animals, he and his team realized that mechanical animals was the only way to go.

Walt would often walk around the park, casually dressed so he would blend in. In the late 1950's and into the early 60's, not everyone knew what Walt looked like. Remember, television was still fairly new then. Walt would walk around Disneyland, checking in on operations and attractions. One day, he rode the Jungle Cruise and, once his ride was over, he angrily stormed off. When he found the manager of Adventureland at the time, Dick Nunis, he asked him how long the Jungle Cruise ride was supposed to be. "Seven minutes," Dick answered. "Well, I just got off a four and a half minute trip," Walt said. "How would you like to go see a movie and they take out a couple of reels in the middle? Do you know how much those animals cost?! I couldn't tell a hippo from an elephant!"

As it turns out, the Jungle Cruise skipper that Walt got that day was on his last day of work at Disneyland and was in a rush to finish his paperwork and get home.

Walt had every Jungle Cruise skipper retrained with a stopwatch to get the ride to EXACTLY seven minutes. Then, instead of riding right after training to make sure they all had it down, Walt waited. He waited for THREE WEEKS, and then he took his stopwatch on a random day and started riding Jungle Cruise boats. He rode one, was happy with the ride time and Skipper's spiel, then moved on to the next boat, and then the next one, riding several boats and experiencing several shows that day to make sure the guest experience was perfect.

And this part doesn't really fit with the rest of the story, but I love it and I want you, if you've read this far and have hung on this far, to know it too! The back of Walt's apartment over the Disneyland Firehouse faced the Jungle Cruise, and Walt would often go outside into the jungle to smoke his cigarettes. Also, Walt's grandchildren have said that they can remember sleeping over in the apartment and hearing the jungle noises all night long! Not great for getting sleep but what a memory!!

"Shoo! Shoo!"

Walt's Temper

It's no secret that Walt Disney had a temper. I haven't talked to anyone who worked for him who didn't love him, but they all have admitted that you didn't want to get in his way on a bad day. He had a couple of tells. If he was listening to you and he was tapping his fingers slowly, that just meant that he was interested. If he was tapping his fingers quickly, that meant he was annoyed and you'd better get to the point, and fast!

I've talked to Bob Gurr an awful lot over the years about Walt. Bob went on and had an entire career after Disney, before coming back to the company, Before I recorded my latest podcast with Bob, I watched a video on YouTube of him telling a story about Walt's famous temper I'd never heard before. I asked him about it during the podcast...

Me: "I saw you tell this story somewhere else, so I needed to ask you about it...someone had you put safety cages on the Rocket Jets, I think this was in the 50's..."

Bob: "(Under his breath, as I'm talking, after a deep breath) Oooooooohhhhhh..."

Me: "And I saw that you told that story at a Town Hall or something and I was wondering if you would tell me if you could?"

Bob: "Uhhh...okay. What we called the Rocket Jet had started out as the Astro Jet and it was actually a stock, German ride. After World War II, the Germans were trying to, you know, get their economy back on line again and there was a company that built these great big bearings, I mean these things were eight or nine feet in diameter...great big ball bearing things? Really expensive! Well, they'd been making them and now the war was over and there are no more German machine guns so what's he gonna do with his bearing factory?

"So he came up with an idea like, 'Well, we'll put an amusement park (ride) in that rotates around like a big Lazy Susan. Okay, now we can sell bearings!' (Laughs) So, this was called

Roto Jets. So the city of Long Beach nearby to Anaheim put in a Roto Jet, and I think that went in there in somewhere in '55, 56 or somewhere in that era. And this was an understandable ride, you know, easy to build, easy to do. But it was physically controlled with an air valve in the cockpit where a person could play around and get it to bounce, In other words, you've got an arm that goes up and down, the car's on it, you can oscillate with air, and a poor lady flipped out and died.

"Yeah, so that was big news in Long Beach, and Joe Fowler said, "Oh, well yeah...the same thing could happen here!" So he says, "My boy," he says...he says, "My boy, I want you to put a safety thing on..." he says..."I want you to do sumpin" (my best transcription of Bob's imitation of Admiral Joe) So I came up with a design that would function automatically...in other words, the ride operator didn't have to do anything extra 'cause it would go up and back down as the booms would go up and back down. So, we didn't have any extra work. It was an ugly thing, but it'd function. Uhh...I got it all working, then I hid it under a staircase under Roger Broggie's office...you know, where nobody'd see it. You know, 'cause it was a job that the Admiral had told me to do and Broggie had said, "Alright, Bob, go ahead and see if you could make it work," which I did.

"And then, I was down at the park like two days later. And Walt, I parked my car and then Walt just pulled up and parked his car, and he was headed straight at me, coming across that parking lot. And he walked up to me and, uh, what's that little thing on your rib cage? What's it called a solar plexus or something like that?"

Me: "Yeah...that's right."

Bob: Yeah...and he was known for hitting people in that...in that tab. And you stopped breathing...I mean, the pain is so bad that you stop breathing. He got my attention! With his finger! And he was in a tirade and basically what he said was, 'I saw that! And it's not going in my park!' Then he hit me (in the chest) again and said, "This is my goddamn park and nothing goes in my goddamn park unless I say it goes in my goddamn park and that's not gonna be in it!" I was powerless to say, "'Joe made me do it! Blame it on the Admiral, Joe Fowler!'

Me: "Did you actually say that?"

Bob: "No! I couldn't say a thing! In the preceding days, Roger Broggie pretended he didn't know a thing about it and the Admiral was always smiling...he always smiled at me...he was nice! He just smiled as if...nothing ever happened! But within ten minutes, Walt was his friendly self...(laughs). But don't ever cross that man."

Don DeFore's Silver Banjo Barbecue

Don DeFore's Silver Banjo Barbecue was the first restaurant in Disneyland to have an actual real live person's name attached to it. I met Don's son, Ron DeFore, at a D23 Expo years ago and asked him if he'd be an early guest on my brand new podcast, the Ear To There Disney Podcast (now known as Turkey Leg Talk). Ron agreed, and we got to talk all about his dad's restaurant and his relationship with Walt Disney.

Ron: "Frito Lay, who had the space where my dad's restaurant eventually went in Frontierland, right next to Aunt Jemima's, they wanted to move because the space was too small. They eventually moved to a space that was more toward the entrance of Frontierland. They needed to fill it with something. By that time, Walt had hired Bud Coulson to be in charge of managing all of the lessees in the park. And so Bud called my dad and said, 'Hey, I remember before you telling me stories about how you know how to cook, and you cooked your way through college, yada yada yada. How would you like to open up a restaurant in Disneyland?'

"And the rest is history. My dad went for it right away. His brother, Vern, managed it. They both had to take a restaurant management course at UCLA. And in 1957 Don DeFore's Silver Banjo Barbecue opened."

Me: "So, you dad didn't have any restaurant experience at all?"

Ron: (Laughs) "Uhh...no." (laughs again) "No, and I'm not sure how much cooking he actually did. I mean, I'm sure he did in college, but nowhere near what a professional chef would do. This really boils down to his relationship with Walt, his relationship with Bud Coulson. As a matter of fact, we've gotten to know Becky Cline (the Director of the Walt Disney Archives) very well and we've met with her numerous times.

"I remember the first time we met with her in Burbank, her commenting on some memos that they had and saying, 'Man, your dad must've been pretty close to Walt. There's no other living human being that ever was allowed to display their name in the park.' My brother (David DeFore) always chimes in, 'Well what about Davy Crockett?' Well, that's where I always qualify it with 'a living human being'! There are others, like Art Linkletter, he owned the Kodak concession, but he was not allowed to display his name. So, the fact that they approved the signage and the sign with my dad's name on it was, as Becky says, a testament to the relationship my dad had with Walt."

I asked Ron why his dad doesn't have a window somewhere on Main Street or somewhere in Frontierland, and he said he and his brother have been pushing for that and bothering Becky Cline about that for years.He then told me about a rogue plan that he and his brother had executed to honor their dad and his restaurant's site in Disneyland on their own.

Ron: "Well there's a funny story about a plaque. There were plaques, plural. When my brother and I do these presentations (for Disney fans), that's kind of the end of the presentation. I don't mind sharing it here with your audience. What it was, was kind of a dream that my brother and I had had for years that they should put a plaque up to commemorate that restaurant, because it is such an unusual, little known part about the park. By the way, the facade for the restaurant is still there. It's still the same. It's unchanged. It's just that it's being used as a storage area for the restaurant next door. It's exactly the same so we were thinking, well, we should put a plaque up there. (I'm going to jump ahead and cut a little out of Ron's story here, just because he talked a bit about Silver Banjo memorabilia collecting and not the plaque) I collected as much (memorabilia) of the Silver Banjo that I could, and I called my brother and said, 'You know what? We're gonna put up a plaque whether Disney wants us to do it or not.'

"So, I researched the appropriate Frontierland font that they would probably use; I'm a wordsmith, by trade, so I sort of figured out what the short little slogan would be if Disney were to put a commemorative plaque up there, and I had it made. I went to a professional company that made brass plaques and we wound up putting it up there! And the way that happened, this was the next Disneyana Convention and someone was doing a book signing and we went over and it was David Mumford and Bob Gordon and the book they had just come out with was *Disneyland: The Nickel Tour.*

"David, when we introduced ourselves, said, 'Oh, my God, I loved interviewing your dad.' And there was an interview (in the book) with my dad that was two pages long all about the Silver Banjo Barbecue, and he said 'Oh, I'm so happy to meet you! That was one of the favorite interviews that I did. Your dad was so nice.' Anyway, I didn't know who David was but I believe at that time he was Vice President of Imagineering and was currently (at that time) a Disney employee. While we're standing there, keep in mind that this was going to be the day that we were going to surreptitiously (Phil here; I had to look this word up. It means secretly) put up a plaque on the facade. And so I'm carrying a bag with this brass plaque, I'm with my brother, I'm with my 80 year old mother who's all ready, willing, and able to do this dirty trick...

"But I'm talking to David Mumford and he's so excited about the history of the park so I said, 'You know what? I know we said we weren't going to tell anybody about this...' but I pulled David aside and I said, 'Look, I'm gonna tell you something, but you have to promise to take off your Disney employee hat and just enjoy it' and he said, 'Sure, what? What are you talking about?' And I said, 'Let me show you what I have in this bag. When we leave here we're walking across the street (to Disneyland) and we're gonna put this up on the facade where the Silver Banjo used to be.' And he looked, and he read the plaque and he totally cracked up, and he said, 'That is fantastic! I won't tell anybody! Good for you guys, and Disney should be doing that themselves. And if they're not, (at least) somebody is!'

"So, fast forward, we're at the park, it's at night, I've got this double stick 'em tape on this plaque, my brother and mother are kind of looking out because there's all kinds of employees around. You know, the bus boy's sweeping the floor and there's a manager and security...and my brother finally just says, 'Go! Do it!' right when the coast was clear. So I stick this thing on and we got all sorts of photos of the three of us standing in front of those French doors that were part of the entrance to the restaurant. We actually got one of the floor sweepers to take a picture of us and I'm sure he had no idea what he was taking a picture of!"

Ron told me that on his way out of Disneyland that day, he was really nervous that he had been caught on camera and a security guard or someone would stop him before he could make a clean getaway. Just as he was walking out of Frontierland back toward Main Street, he heard someone shout, "Stop!" He felt a hand on his back. He turned to see David Mumford and about 7 or 8 of his Disney cast member friends. The last photo Ron had taken that day was of that plaque with himself, his mom, his brother, and a bunch of Disney cast members and higher ups who were in the know!

That plaque stayed up for quite a while. Months after Ron had surreptitiously installed it, he was talking to a Disneyland cast member friend who had told him that, in an operating manual somewhere in Disneyland, there was now a full page dedicated to "How to Care for and Maintain the Don DeFore Silver Banjo Barbecue Plaque."

Walt & the Sunkist House

Way back before it was the Gibson Girl Ice Cream Parlor, the storefront next to the Penny Arcade on Main Street, U.S.A. in Disneyland was the Sunkist Citrus House. In the early 1960s, this store was owned and operated by Sunkist, not by Walt Disney or Disneyland.

Walt was an early riser. On mornings when he would wake up in his apartment above the firehouse in Town Square, he would stroll down to the Citrus House and "break in" to use the cool, new juicing machines. Eventually the manager at the Sunkist House had an electric juicer added to Walt's countertop appliances in his apartment which sat right next to his electric sandwich press. Like the big kid he was, Walt kept breaking in, even though he had the countertop juicer. He told the manager of the Citrus House that the juice from the juicer 'just didn't taste the same.'

The manager of the Sunkist Citrus House asked Walt's secretary to always give him the heads up when Walt was going to be in the park to make sure there were enough oranges for both him and the guests! This leads to a story I first told maybe three weeks ago, but I'm going to tell it again, just because it fits so well here with the oranges! If you read this one already, you can stop here!

On one night in the early 1960s, overnight workers in Disneyland were replacing the horse drawn trolley tracks. It was about 3am, and they had been using jackhammers for hours, pulling the old trolley track out to install a new one, when a worker noticed that Walt was sitting on a bench across from them in Town Square, eating an orange.

"Sorry, Mr. Disney! We didn't know you were sleeping here. We'll keep it down!" Walt responded, "No, it's much more important for the tracks to be ready when the guests arrive tomorrow morning than it is for me to get a few hours sleep! Want an orange?"

And that is how, according to the late Rolly Crump and his *Walk Through the Park with Rolly Crump*, some overnight Disneyland workers had the chance to sit on a bench in Disneyland and share oranges with Walt Disney at 3am sometime in the early 1960s!

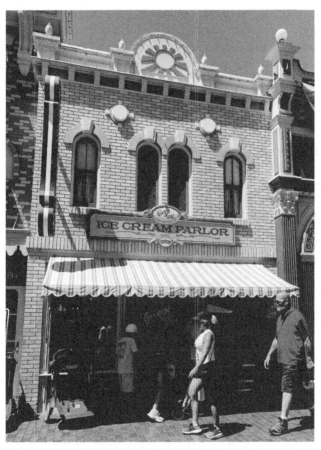

The Gibson Girl Ice Cream Parlor, formerly The Sunkist House, the site of Walt's late night orange thefts.

Disneyland's First Private Club

It's widely accepted that the first private club built where Walt
Disney would entertain guests was Club 33 in New Orleans
Square, but that's not really true. Walt did design Club 33 for
visiting VIPs, business associates, and friends but he didn't
live to see it completed. He did, however, entertain those
important to him at the Red Wagon Inn on Main Street USA.

Before it was renovated and renamed the Plaza Inn in 1965
(after the Disney company bought out all of the third party
restaurant vendors), The Red Wagon Inn was Walt's favorite
Disneyland restaurant. It was the only one that served a full
course dinner in the park at the time and was actually made up
of three dining areas: the main dining area that guests could
access, the "in between" room that was for cast member meals
(and a nod to "in-betweeners in animation"), and a private,
secret dining area in the rear of the restaurant known as The
Hideaway.

Emile Kuri was called upon again to salvage everything
he could from an opulent 1870s mansion in Los Angeles that
Walt purchased as it was set to be demolished. Those pieces
were used all over Disneyland with the most impressive items
saved for the Red Wagon Inn, including the giant stained glass
ceiling and beautiful leaded cut-glass entrance doors.

Guests would need to know where to access the secret
entrance for The Hideaway in order to get in. The room featured a fully stocked bar (the only one in Disneyland at the
time) and a private restroom. Walt frequently entertained
friends, family, VIPs, and more in his secret little restaurant!

The Viewliner and Why It Went Away So Quickly

Here's what Bob Gurr told me about one of the shortest-lived Disneyland attractions, The Viewliner.

"It goes back to...one day, Roger Broggie, my boss, and Truman Woodworth, the manager of the park, were walking by the Phantom Boats, which never did work, and we had a body of water out there. Okay...so Woody says, 'Well, Walt's got everything here, almost, except for a submarine.' Well, two weeks later I was asked to start designing a submarine!

"Okay, so that's the way things start out. Then, similarly about that time, we had a circus north of Autopia that didn't work. So now we had a vacant lot. So, the next thing was, Walt wanted to throw a Junior Autopia out there. And then in that same conversation he just happened to say, 'Yeah, we need to have something else out there. We should put in a railroad. Our guy Tony who knows how to lay the track; we just tell him where we wanna put it and he just goes out. You know, a railroad is just a couple of rails, some ballast, some spikes and all that kinda stuff. Oh, and by the way, Bobby here will design a train for it.'"

Me: "But at this point you had never done a train..."

Bob: "Ummm, no!! I had never done a train!" (Laughing)

Me: "Right, right, right. But you're just gonna do it."

Bob: "Okay...yeah! Just in passing, he just says that, so my boss, Roger Broggie Senior, said, 'Okay, get started.' It was going to be an extremely fast development job. In fact, that's something I'm going to be making a movie about later this year: how did Walt get people to do high speed, fast development jobs, that when you were done, they looked professional, but they were built using junkyard parts?

"Okay, that meant we'd have a streamlined train. Okay. They'd already set the gauge for the track, which I think was

30 inch, so a narrow track. So we knew the size of about what the train should be and we knew the turning radius and all that kinda stuff. So I thought, 'Oh boy, I liked the General Motors Train of Tomorrow that used to run between L.A. and Las Vegas a few years earlier that was designed by General Motors. It was a lightweight train with a big locomotive that had a wraparound windshield that looked absolutely terrific. I knew the designed that had designed it. So, anyway, I thought, 'If you're gonna steal, steal from the best!'

So I took that basic design and I thought, 'Oh my gosh, do you know how much work it is to design doors, windshields, and all that sort of stuff?' So I said, 'You know, with that size, I think a General Motors A Body, which is a Chevy, Pontiac, Oldsmobile or small Buick, and a four door, would give me the short door and a wraparound windshield and on the Oldsmobile it would give me an interior that I could swap out the right to left because train drivers drive on the right...they don't drive on the left.'

So I went to a local junkyard and I looked around and I said, 'I'm looking for a '54 Oldsmobile four door.' And he says, 'Yeah! We got one out in the back! Lady got killed in it, but, uh, the cab is okay.' 'So yeah, I said, 'I'll take it.' It was only about one hundred and fifty bucks. And I said, 'Well, I need two' and he said, 'I'll call you in a couple weeks.' And he called like a week later and said, 'Well, I got another one.' So, anyway, for three hundred bucks I have two Oldsmobile bodies. So we chop up what we don't need and I have doors for the vehicle and all the surrounding stuff is just complicated stuff...the instrument panel, the windshield, it's all so complicated. Now I have all the complicated stuff for three hundred bucks for two trains. Okay.

"Now, all I have to do is design that streamlined front end on it. Okay. Well, I know a guy who does Indianapolis race car bodies and he was busy in '57, so he said 'I'll get to it in a couple weeks.' Then I go down to Cal Metal Shaping in L.A. and we make a wood buck of the shape of it, you know all the forms. And we get California Metal shaping to hammer out enough of the shapes of the parts so that Mike Scott, the Indianapolis race car guy, he can put it all together and ship it up to us in Burbank and we'll weld it onto the Oldsmobile."

I'm jumping ahead in the story here. Bob got super technical with all the ins and outs and electricity this and that. Basically, he butted heads with the folks who he worked on the design of the Viewliner with, which isn't surprising because Bob will admit he often butted heads with those in charge. The Viewliner, after some trial and error and a smokey cabin with Walt riding and the Disneyland Band playing on its Opening Day, went on to have a short but pretty problem-free operation history. Bob continued, about Walt:

"So why did he want that little train (built) so fast? He never told us that he already had the 1959 all new Tomorrowland in mind. Whoa. He wanted something temporary, so that's why it had a short life. It was deliberately intentioned to just have anything out in the back where there was a dead circus, a vacant lot, and a little Junior Autopia that had nothing around it. So, all of a sudden, with that kind of move of building an Autopia track and we had a waterway now because we already had a pond for the boats that didn't work, so here we are! We've got attractions out in the back now so there's more stuff, but to get ready for the big stuff which was monorail, submarine, Matterhorn."

Rolly Crump's Propellers and Dope Posters

The late Imagineer Rolly Crump once made some waves at the Disney Studio by creating some fun "dope posters" that were meant as a joke. He designed posters for pretend products like cocaine candy and marijuana cigarettes that were imported by "Stoned and Co." He told me a great story about how those and some other creations of his got the attention of the "Ol' Maestro" himself.

Me: "When you were working in animation, I read that you really caught Walt's eye with some propellers you designed that you had in your office that you would set up?"

Rolly: "That's a beautiful story because it changed my life. There was an animator I was working for, and I went in to have my scene checked, Wathel Rogers was his name, and he had this little clip on a push pin on a little lamp that he had, and the little clip was spinning around like a propeller. So I asked Wathel, I said, 'God, that's really neat! How'd you do that?' He says, 'It's a secret.' So I went back, and these little clips came off of the erasers of the pencils that we were using, and so I tried making a propeller, and I don't know how many pencils I screwed up trying to make the propeller but I couldn't get it to work.

"And so I went back to Wathel and I said, 'Please, Wathel, tell me how you did that.' And so I drove him crazy for a while and he finally said, 'I'll tell you what, Rolly. I'll sell it to you.' So he sold it to me for a penny. So, when I got the little clip, I found out the reason I was making a mistake with the clips was, I was using a nail to make the dent, which meant that it was a crooked little dent. And what he'd use was a ballpoint pen, so it was a smooth little dent. So that's how I learned to make these little propellers.

"So I got really excited about it and little by little I started building all kinds of little propellers. And I had my office filled with about thirty of them, and that's how I got started. A good friend of mine at Animation said, 'You know, Rolly, you should have an exhibit in the library with your propellers.' Well, the library was used, kind of, as a little art gallery and different people that worked in Animation would have an art show in there. And I went to the little gal that ran it and she said, 'Yeah, Rolly, we'd love to have a show with your propellers.'

"So I did all my propellers and I had some paintings that I did, and then down the hallway I did a whole series of posters, which were my dope posters, my marijuanas and my "Cocaine Candies" and everything. Well, the head librarian called me and she says, 'Walt came in and saw your show today.' And I said, 'Oh my God!' She said, 'Yeah!' She said, 'He really liked the propellers.' I said, 'Did he go down the hallway where all the dope posters were?!'

"She says, 'Yeah!' I said, 'Well, what did he say?' And she says, 'He laughed.' And I thought, 'Oh my God...he understands my little posters were kind of a gag. So, that's how it all got started. Walt saw my propellers there, and it wasn't until years later, when we were working on the World's Fair, that he asked me to design the Tower of the Four Winds."

Bob Gurr's Fire Engine

All of the Main Street Vehicles that you can currently ride in Disneyland were Walt Disney's original ideas except for one, the Disneyland Fire Engine. Bob Gurr told me the story a few years ago about how he kind of snuck that one by Walt.

"I wanted a fire engine and I knew I would never have enough money to get one. One day Walt was in my office and in the same manner that he had come in a couple of years before, Walt had slapped his knee and said, 'You know what we don't have on Main Street, Bobby? We don't have a double decker omnibus...why don't you get started on one?' Well, I did the same thing to him in early 1958. I slapped my knee and I said, 'Say Walt? You know what we don't have on Main Street USA? We don't have a fire engine. We had a horse-drawn one in the old days, you know, but it wasn't practical.' And Walt said, 'Yeah, you're right. We don't.'

"He left and about 20 minutes later my phone rings and I answer and it's the accounting department and they say, 'Walt was just here and here's the project number so you can get started on the fire engine. I said, YAHOO! I'm gonna have a fire engine!"

Bob built the fire engine on the studio lot in Burbank and actually got to drive it down the Santa Ana Freeway all the way to Anaheim and Main Street USA, where it has been ever since!

Bob Gurr Designs the Monorail

Bob Gurr told me:

"If you look really close at the original Herb Ryman drawing, the lower right hand corner where there's the Tomorrowland-like place; behind the building you'll see a monorail which is the hanging type, the one that hangs from, you know, a beam or a track or a rail up in the sky. Most people looked at it and they didn't even see that.

"So Walt had this idea in mind and then in 1958 he and his wife, Lilly, were driving on this little road in Cologne, Germany, and this monorail goes right across the roadway, right above him, and disappears through these trees. Now he'd seen a monorail so he immediately went over and started talking to 'em (the Alweg Company; designers of that monorail) and started negotiations within just a couple days.

"Then Walt came in my office and gave me these pictures of this pretty ugly-lookin' railroad car that looked like a loaf of bread with a slot in the bottom that was sitting on a stick. It really was, I mean...I wouldn't have done something like that. The front end looked like an old World War II German bomber, actually. And all Walt said, he left me the pictures, and he left me a couple of technical drawings of how the thing worked, you know, it's called a German Saddlebag Beamway. And he said, 'Now Bobby, I want you to get started on this. Work with your boss, he'll get you some more help. Get started.'

"So, in a matter of a couple of days I could see the problem of the appearance of the train; this loaf of bread sittin' on a stick. I thought, 'We have to hide that slot.' It's like a camouflage job, what can I do to do that? So I came up with the idea of the pointed vehicle, like a Buck Rogers spaceship. But if you look at that old Buck Rogers spaceship, it had these splayed fins like a kids' sled, so it would slide to a halt on the planet and it was all very fantasy. But I thought, 'You know? That would be a good way to hide that slot!' We'd still have the same slot, of course, but your eye would be drawn to the pointed nose and these lower splayed side fins, and then I made the body kinda roundy, so it splayed out a bit, and that made the thing not look so tall.

"Then, of course, you have the wrap around windshield, and you put the bubble canopy on the top like it's a B-47 bomber, and those are the elements. That fell into place with no other sketches. I just went straight to what I thought the answer was. I made a quick sketch on my kitchen table one morning and then when I got to the office I made a rendering of it and that rendering is the thing you see all the time whenever you see that piece titled "Monorail Crossing." I made the picture and Disney artist John Hench put the color on it." "Well, Walt came over to take a look at the thing, and he took one look at it and said, 'Bobby...can you build that?' And I says, 'Yeah.' And he smiled and walked out and that was it. That was the approval process!"

Bob Gurr's monorails, still riding the same rails in Disneyland in 2024.

Building Walt's Submarine Fleet

I once asked Bob Gurr how he came up with his ideas. He tried to change the topic and said he never had an original idea or concept. He said Walt Disney or others would come to him with the idea, and he'd turn their idea into a concept drawing or sketch. I didn't let him get away with that and said he was being modest and he came up with the look of the Disneyland Monorail which looked COMPLETELY different than the monorail Walt Disney had shown him in a photo (among a million other things). After that, he explained what it was like creating stuff.

Bob: "There are a bunch of kinds of people I've run across in every kind of trade, you know whether it's automotive, space-craft, or particularly aircraft...umm, they just see things in their minds. It just...the ideas appear. And you can't...you can't design fast enough! In other words, you never stall. You're never in a position where you say to yourself, 'Oh, how are we going to figure this out?' It's the other way around. It's like, 'Oh, this would be so cool! Boy, there's a half a dozen ways we could do this so I gotta figure which one will be the fastest, quickest way to do this!'

"You have so many ideas that look like they might work versus the guy that sits there and says, 'They want us to do a what? How in the world are we ever gonna do that?!' They (the first guy) has no fear of treading into this stuff because there are just so many possibilities!"

Me: "See, Bob, I hear you say this stuff...but how does Walt Disney come to you (a guy who hasn't built a submarine) and say, 'I need a submarine for my submarine ride in Disneyland' and you...like, how does that work? How do you figure out, 'Okay, this is how we're going to keep the water out?' How does that work? I don't understand how your mind works and how you can do that."

Bob: "Oh well, in the case of that one, I was walkin' alongside the old Phantom Boat River, where we built the little Viewliner train and Truman Woodward, the manager of the park, and (Roger) Broggie and I were walkin' there and Woody says, 'You know, Walt's got everything in this park except he doesn't have a submarine.' And within about ten days, Roger comes to me and he says, uh, 'Walt wants you to get started on the submarine project.' And that's how quickly an idea started.

"And so right away Admiral Fowler, who managed the park also, he said, 'Oh, well I have somebody in the Todd Shipyard in Los Angeles that can build it as soon as we come up with a design.' And then, 'Oh, I know a diesel engine company we could buy one from, the MAN Company.' Then somebody else said, 'Well, Bob, all you gotta do is figure out how to submerge it.' It's only gotta go down about three feet. So I went and looked at books about how submarines worked and I could see, 'Oh yeah, you've got a buoyancy thing, you know, water goes in and out of the thing, then you've gotta displace water, you know? I mean, it's just plain, ordinary math.' And then somebody else said, 'Oh, you wanna run it on a cable drive system like (the name of a German amusement park I could not understand or make out), in Germany.'

"So, Roger and I got up to San Francisco and the manger of the cable car company says, 'Okay, I'll take you out for the day so that I can show you why you'd never use cables to drive anything. It's just ridiculous!' So, these were the opinions! So drawing from all that I figure, 'Well, it oughta be about this big and it oughta look like that. The Nautilus Atomic Submarine had just popped up in the Arctic a year or two before and I thought, 'Well, that's simple. What's the best way to see it (the show)? Well, a porthole! Everybody sticks their head in a porthole. Well, we'll just sit them on little benches or something like that. Well, there's seats on either side, so there's a show on both sides. Okay, what's the best way to get into the boat? Oh, spiral staircases! They're really compact! So, you see, in a couple of minutes, the configuration of the boat solved itself!"

Yeah, sure, Bob! it just designed itself. It didn't have anything to do with going to the library and teaching yourself how submarines worked before building a darn submarine!

Bob's Proudest Moment & Earl Vilmer

I asked Bob Gurr, "What was your proudest moment while working for the Disney Company?"

Bob: "Ohhhh, there's about ten thousand of 'em!"

Me: "Okay, well, can you maybe share one or two, then?"

Bob: "I'd have to answer it this way: every time we did something and Walt was happy with it and he had a smile on his face as he was talking to an important guest, just like the Cheshire Cat like, 'I just ate the bird, wanna see the feathers?' It was kind of his general attitude. And then I would have to say the monorail, I think it was the night before the opening with the Nixon thing, the next day.

"Nobody else drove that train except me. We didn't have time to even train them on it. So I drove it all the time. You know, I'd drive it like one lap and it would break or something. But we had a railroad guy named Earl Vilmer who was very conservative, railroad, old school and he was such a steam engine guy that the monorail, to him, was so advanced, and it was in his area of maintenance responsibility. And as I drove the train for the first time at night I remember going up over the top of the waterfall and then I heard this quiet voice on the radio, with no call, I just heard these words, 'Ah, a thing of beauty!' And that kind of, that kind of lasted with me forever."

Me: "That's cool."

Bob: "Because it came from a guy who was from a previous century."

Me: "Sure. A guy who probably was not ready to embrace the technology of an electric train."

Bob: "That's exactly right. So that one...that one sticks out."

Bob Gurr Kidnaps Vice President Nixon

On June 14, 1959, Bob Gurr kidnapped Vice President Richard Nixon. Bob told me all about it on one episode of my podcast, Turkey Leg Talk.

"We were building the monorail and two weeks before we were gonna dedicate it, we had the train set on the beam way. And in that two weeks we finished settling it and testing it and it broke down every day, except for the day before the dedication. We were also gonna have a live, 30 minute, black and white TV program and the monorail had to perform for the ribbon cutting.

"So I parked the monorail right at the platform, rather than taking it back to the the service area, 'cause I knew that if we were gonna have live television, to get their shot, all I had to do was drive it away far enough that it's out of the shot and then it can go break down again and it'd be okay. That was the plan but at about 11 o'clock in the morning on a really hot day, here comes Walt and he's got security with him and, oh God, he's got the Vice President of the United States, his wife, their two girls, some Secret Service guys. And Walt wanted to show off something he had that no one else had.

"So he came up and took a look at the train and said, 'Well, Bobby, let's go inside it.' I said, 'Just give me a few minutes. I've gotta turn the air-conditioning on, because it's pretty hot!' So, as soon as it got cooled down I opened the door and we all piled into the cab and Walt introduces everybody all the way around. See, Nixon's a good friend of his, he calls him Dick...so, anyway, he says, 'You know, Dick, I'm the steam guy. I drive the steam locomotives here, but this is new, advanced, modern electric transportation so I have Bobby drive it!' (on the podcast, I inserted a "Lightbulb" noise because Bob's face lit up and he smiled with this memory) Pause. I just took off!

"Yeah I drove off and in those days, the train would go out and make a right turn and then make a left turn and then come back around over the sub ride, which meant that Nixon could see that on the load platform, all the Secret Service guys were there, I think there were four or five of them, they're there which means no Secret Service are on the train. Presidents always want to escape their Secret Service deal but they never can escape. It's just one of those things they all want to do and none of them ever do it. And, apparently Nixon caught on very quickly that he was successful, that he escaped the Secret Service. Of course, he let out some four letter words which I can't repeat!

"And then we got back to the platform and I thought, 'Oh, God, I gotta stop back where that ribbon is gonna go.' And then the girls said, 'Let's go again! Let's go again!' So Walt said, "Give 'em another ride!' At this point the Secret Service guys are running toward the train as it pulls back into the station. Bob has said they then ran alongside it as it sped up and left the station again!

"I can't even remember that second lap around. I was so heartsick that we were gonna miss that shot and the ribbon cutting. And, besides, if it catches on fire again and we're over the sub ride, we don't have the evacuation ladders or anything and we'd burn that President up...of course, that would've saved him all of that Watergate stuff later!"

Everyone made it back to the platform safely with no fires and no incidents. The Secret Service finally caught back up with Vice President Nixon and his family and, as Bob was walking the platform of his brand new monorail, he was approached by a furious German Alweg Monorail Engineer, named Conrad.

Bob: "Mr. Bob! (this is now Bob speaking with a German accent like Hogan's Heroes) In Germany at Alweg, we spent seven years and seven million marks to develop the monorail and we never let the public on it and you stupid Disney people, you get it running one day and you put your Vice President on it?!' And he was furious and I said, 'Conrad, this is the Disney Way!'"

Rock Candy Mountain

Once Disneyland's Matterhorn Mountain was built, Walt Disney was itching to add yet another mountain to his expanding park. According to Harriet Burns, he said, "Now that we've done a mountain we know how to do the structure, we can have another mountain over here. Every kid dreams of a mountain of candy; I did when I was a kid, we can have a candy mountain, nothing but candy."

Walt had Herb Ryman draw the original concept for Rock Candy Mountain, and he tasked Harriet and her fellow Imagineers Fred Joerger and Claude Coats, with turning Herb's sketches into a three dimensional model. The team built a one-inch scale model of the mountain, which ended up being quite large. The size of the model allowed for the Imagineers to use actual, regular sized candy to landscape the mountain. Claude Coats went to a local grocery store by the studio and bought out all of the candy that they had in the store. Lollipops, candy canes, gum drops, you name it, he bought it. It wasn't enough. Candy was ordered from factories across California and glued to the mountain.

Walt would come by and visit the three of them often. He had a lot of input on the look and style of the mountain, as he did with all of the early Disneyland attractions. He told Harriet, "I know we'll have a waterfall here, we can have raspberry falls, and then we can sell raspberry popsicles or raspberry juice at the bottom, we can have lemonade falls on the other side and do the same." Changes were made according to Walt's input, and the team of three kept chugging along.

There was a giant door in the room that led directly to the outside. This was great for the Imagineers, as they could have trucks drive right into the room to make deliveries. It wasn't great for Rock Candy Mountain, however. Crows discovered the sheer volume of candy and peanuts that was stuck to the mountain, and would routinely dive bomb into the room, stealing whatever they could before being chased back outside. Now, I've mentioned John Hench a bunch in these stories the last couple of months. John was Walt's guy and Walt really, really respected his opinion. Walt asked John to come down to the room to take a look at the progress of Rock Candy Mountain. He wanted him to give an honest assessment of the concept. John walked into the room, walked around the model, apparently grimaced and said, "Well Walt when you have a meal of meat and potatoes, you really enjoy a dessert of candy, but when you just see piles, and piles, and piles of it, it kind of turns you off."

Walt looked at John for a moment, then said, "You know, you're right, just forget the whole thing." The giant door was opened and the entire model was pushed outside into the trash for the birds and squirrels to enjoy!

Thank you so much for reading this one! I'm in a Harriet Burns mood since it was her birthday yesterday, but I've been sitting on this one for a while, waiting to tell it! The quotes come from an interview with Harriet Burns from *Tomart's Disneyana Update*, the photo of Harriet on the model comes from Disney and the archives, and the Rock Candy Mountain tribute photo was taken by a friend of mine at DCA.

Lillian's Anniversary Gift

It was late in the evening on July 11, 1956, when Walt Disney and his wife, Lillian, spotted the sign for Pike's Petrified Forest as they were driving through the mountains near Colorado Springs. Walt took the next exit and pulled up outside the attraction right around closing time. Walt got out of the car to explore and a young boy approached him, telling Walt that it was getting dark and the views of the forest wouldn't be very good. Walt said he didn't mind and handed over the 35 cents, the cost of admission. Lillian stayed in the car.

Walt was gone for a while. A really long while. As the legend goes, Walt knew Lilly would be a little annoyed with him for leaving her in the car for so long, especially since it was very close to their wedding anniversary. When Walt got back to the car he tried to smooth it over with a little joke. He told Lilly, "Honey, I bought you an anniversary present."

The "anniversary present" was a 55 million year old, ten foot high, five ton petrified tree stump that Walt purchased from the owner of Pike's Petrified Forest for $1,650. He actually had written a check for it and arranged for it to be delivered back to California before he returned to the car.

For years, the story was that the tree was actually given to Lillian by Walt and it sat in their backyard until Lilly got tired of it and donated it to Disneyland, where it's been ever since. What was kind of lost in that story was the humor, or the gag, that Walt was always going for, even in his family life. In 2010, Walt and Lillian's daughter, Diane Disney Miller, had this to say about the story: "Of course it was staged, and it is very playful on both of their parts. The 'gift to my wife' was just a gag. He was the consummate gag man, and proud of it."

Running Carousel of Progress Joke

On my podcast, Turkey Leg Talk, I mentioned to Bob Gurr that I didn't know he had worked on the Carousel of Progress. That was kind of a silly thing to say, because I knew that he had worked on all four New York World's Fair attractions. I had just forgotten. After he made fun of me for never paying attention when he talks, he told me this fun story about it.

"We were mocking up some of the acts, in full size, in one of our MAPO buildings (MAPO, which stood for Mary Poppins, was the manufacturing area of WED, which eventually became Walt Disney Imagineering)...you know, where we had the room to build stuff. So, we set up a stage for, say, Act I, II, III, IV, etc. And then we had all the animated, you know, we had the mother and the father and the kids and all that kind of stuff; Uncle Orville in the bathtub and all that stuff.

Original concept model of the Carousel of Progress from the Walt Disney Family Museum in San Francisco.

"And Walt comes over every day or so and he's refining it, and we're all standing around and then he characteristically says, 'Say, Bobby, what if'...it's what if, it was always WHAT IF...'what if we had a little dog? And we put the dog on the stage...but as we change scenes over the years, it was a different dog every time...but the dog was sittin' in the same place?' And he says, 'What if we program the dog so that he's always looking at the same seat?' And he says, "That way, the poor guy that sits in that seat...when the theater rotates, every twenty or thirty years in history, the damn dog barks at the same guy!'

"So, remember, it turns out by Act III the Father was sitting there and he had to tell him (the dog), 'Rover! Leave him alone!' So I got to make this cute little dog. He didn't have to do much, he just wagged his tail and he had to turn around, he had a big neck move. He had to respond to his owner but he had to turn and bark at the guy in the seat. It was a running gag!"

They'll Poop in the Food

Lillian Disney was a big antique collector. She would often drag Walt to antique shops when they were away in a new town or on vacation. On one of those vacations in the late 1940s, Walt accompanied his wife to an antique shop in the French Quarter in New Orleans. While there, Walt spotted an antique golden birdcage with a singing bird inside it. Fascinated, he purchased it, brought it back to his studio, and tasked some folks there with figuring out how the movements worked.

That idea never left Walt's imagination. Some of the earliest animated figures that were put into Disneyland, like the animals throughout the Jungle Cruise, were inspired by that singing bird. In 1961, Walt was adding new things to his park. One of those things was to be a restaurant, sponsored by Stouffer's, which was one of the biggest restaurant chains in the country at the time (and didn't just make frozen food, which I found out very recently). In the earliest plans, it was known as the "Bird Cafe" or "Tiki Gardens." This, of course, was the early concept for the Enchanted Tiki Room.

Rolly Crump said, "Walt always wanted a tea room, but instead we were gonna do a little restaurant. John Hench was asked to do a rendering. And in there, he had birds in cages. Walt took one look at it and he said, 'John, you can't have birds in cages.' John said, 'Why not?' And Walt said, 'Because they'll poop in the food.' That's exactly what he said. We all cracked up and John says, 'No, no, no. Maybe they're little mechanical bids?' And Walt said, 'Oh, little mechanical birds?' And that's how it all got started."

I'll skip ahead a couple of years in this story for the sake of time. The entire Enchanted Tiki Room attraction was built on a soundstage. Walt would bring guests and friends and family in to see it. They would sit in the chairs and Walt's Imagineers would play the show for them, and almost everyone had the same reaction. They would say something like, "Wow, Walt!

That was amazing! What is it?" Walt wasn't happy with their reactions. Something was missing.

When one half of his favorite songwriting duo, Richard Sherman came by to see it, he had a similar reaction: "Walt, it's wonderful! What is it?" Walt said, "That's what you guys are going to write a song about. You're going to explain what this thing is all about!" And that was how the Sherman Brothers got started on the first ever audio-animatronic song, "The Tiki Tiki Tiki Tiki Tiki Room."

Walt Disney's Enchanted Tiki Room - Poop Free Since 1963!

Rolly and the Tiki Room Pre Show

Rolly Crump designed some classic attractions in Disneyland and Walt Disney World including it's a small world & Mr. Toad's Wild Ride, but he might be best-known for his numerous contributions to Walt Disney's Enchanted Tiki Room. I had the chance to talk to him for almost two hours several years ago on my podcast, and he and his wife Marie were literally two of the kindest people I've ever spoken to. This story comes from Rolly since he tells it best.

"I was very fortunate to be asked by Walt to design all of the pre-show tikis that went in there. Now, the Tiki Room had been originally designed as a restaurant. They wanted a Tahitian restaurant in Adventureland and so they though, well, let's do one, and the background could be tikis. So Walt felt that when people were waiting in line that he wanted something to kind of entertain them before they went in to eat. He didn't want them just standing out there. So he asked me if I would design some pre-show tikis that would entertain them before they went in.

"So, I did. I got a book out of the library called *The Whispers on the Wind* that was written by missionaries that had been out to the islands of the Pacific and had documented all of the different beliefs that the Islanders had about their tikis. So I got the list of the tikis and started developing; I did some sketches of 'em and Pele was one of 'em, he's the God of Volcanoes. And then we had the God of the East Winds, we had Rongo who was the God of Agriculture, so I developed all these little sketches of tikis and I showed them to Walt and Walt said, 'Great, Rolly. We'll have these and we'll have some dialogue written and we'll actually have the tikis talk to the public while the people are waiting there.' So I said, 'Okay, that's great.'

"So I went to Blaine Gibson who was our head sculptor, and I said, 'Blaine, Walt wants to get these sculpted.' And Blaine says, 'I can't. I don't have the time.' Actually Blaine was our

*Rolly Crump's previously unnamed Maui sculpture
still welcomes guests to this day.*

only sculptor at the time. So I said, 'Who is gonna sculpt
them?' He said, 'You are!' I said, 'I am? I've never sculpted one
thing in my life!' And he said, 'Well, you're gonna sculpt now!'
So Blaine taught me how to build the armature (the metal
framework on which the clay is molded), how to put the clay
on, and how to sculpt."

When Rolly first got started sculpting on his own, the air con-
ditioned studio was much to cool and the clay wouldn't get soft
enough to mold. Rolly took the clay outside to the WED Cafe
parking lot and sculpted in the sun. He had forgotten some
fine sculpting tools, so he used plastic cutlery from the cafe to
carve and sculpt the finer lines of the tikis.

"The interesting thing about it is, the first one I did (sculpted), Maui, that's the one that's spitting water into a bamboo tube... now, the cute thing about Maui is he also has the sun setting over his head. Well the sketch that I did did not have a sun over his head. I did all of these sketches and there was Rongo and all of the others and they all had real titles, but this was just a sketch I did of one spitting water into the bamboo and then letting the bamboo dump it, but it wasn't really a tiki and I didn't give it a title and Walt asked me, he said 'Are all of these tikis authentic tikis?' And I said, 'Yes, sir'. And he said, 'Well, what's that one the God of?' and he was pointing at the one spitting water into the bamboo. I didn't have A CLUE what to say!

"Luckily, John Hench was standing next to me and he said, 'Well, Walt It's the god of tapa cloth beating.' And Walt didn't quite understand what John said; John had said tapa cloth, and Walt thought he had said clock. So Walt asked John, 'Is he a clock??!' And John said, 'Yes, it's the god that tells the time!' After the meeting was over, John took me aside and he said, 'Rolly, you better go find out who the god of telling time is!'"

The Gags in the Animation Building

A few years ago I had the absolute pleasure of having Disney animator Floyd Norman on my podcast, Turkey Leg Talk. I asked him all about the practical jokes and gags that Rolly Crump had told me about years prior, including the day that Rolly had driven his motorcycle down the hallway of a building at the Disney Studio. Here's what Floyd had to say about the pranks and parties in the 50s and 60s at the Disney Studio.

"Well, the studio was well known—when you've got a creative enterprise like Disney with a bunch of madcap cartoonists, you can expect, uh...(laughs) a degree of trouble. All in good fun. There was never anything done that was injurious to people or...(laughs again)...nobody got hurt, for the most part! Except, at a party one guy, one animator fell out of a second story window (laughs even harder).

"But, he wasn't injured because, thankfully, he landed on a tree. At that particular party, I wasn't there, but I was told that somebody even galloped a horse down the hallway; something more dramatic than riding a motorcycle, I think!

"But, yeah, there were always these madcap gags and fun goings on. One guy had a convertible in the Disney Studio parking lot and I was told that somebody turned it into a bathtub by filling the interior of the car with water! (laughs again) So there were outrageous pranks going on and I think the fun part of all of this is that Walt Disney recognized that this was all part of, you know, having a bunch of cartoonists on your payroll. That they were gonna do outrageous and outlandish things. And that if you were going to run this kind of a business, you pretty much better get used to having a bunch of half-crazy people working for you. Because that's what it required."

Rolly's Gag on the Janitors

What was it like working in animation at the Disney Studio in the 1950s and 1960s? I asked Rolly Crump that on my podcast, Turkey Leg Talk.

"There was quite a group of us. It was almost like being in college; the whole studio lot was like a campus. We became very close, almost like family. Working in animation was absolutely a delight because of all of the different guys I worked with. In fact, I mentioned that to Walt one time. He asked me where I had learned everything and I said, 'Well, I learned it from you.' He said, 'Whatta ya mean, you learned it from me?' And I said, 'Because I was in so many different rooms and I worked with so many different artists, I learned from every one that I was in a room with.' Which was really true, it was an absolutely incredible time frame."

I also asked Rolly about the pranks that he and other animators used to play on one another.

"We used to play gags on each other every day and one of the favorite gags that we had was we would tape down the buttons on the phone, so whoever answered the phone, it would keep ringing. We did that to a little guy who came to work for us from South America and he absolutely started screaming and threw the phone down and ran out the door! (Laughs) Then we would have rubber band fights because all the scenes came in these big, red rubber bands, so sometimes in the evening when we were working overtime we'd start shooting each other!"

My favorite prank Rolly pulled was on the custodians who were in charge of cleaning the room where he and Yale Gracey worked each day, coming up with illusions for the Haunted Mansion.

"We got a call one day and we had this big room that was all blocked off, and it was black (dark, I think). And in there we had all of this stuff. We had these masks that we had gotten in a magic shop in Hollywood that we were gonna use for some of our illusions and we also built a huge monster...and Walt came in and saw it and we had a rat trap that we used that would go off with an infrared gun, and it would blow its (the monster's) head off...the whole thing would blow up and fall down. And we were just doing crazy stuff like that. And Walt came in there and he took the gun, he shot the guy, he blew up and everything.

"And so, we found out later, we got a call from personnel and they said, 'The janitors do not want to come into your office unless you leave all the lights on.' They didn't wanna come in there and see all those skulls and all those funny heads and stuff. So we said, 'Okay.'

"So Yale rigged the room. He had an infrared beam in there right in the middle of the room and he turned the lights real low, was the way it was set up. And my wife had made a silk ghost that had a twelve inch fan underneath it and when you'd turn it on the ghost would blow up and shimmer and shake. Then, of course, we had the monster and all of these other heads and stuff. Well, we set the room up where the light was low so that when the janitors came in, that was the trigger, and that would turn the light off and all of the black lights on and the ghost would come to life and the big guy would blow up and his head would go all over the room...you know, on a string.

"So, sure enough we went home and the next day we came in and the head was hanging in the middle of the room and the ghost was still up there shimmering and shaking...(laughs). We got a call a little later that morning and they said, 'The janitors are never coming back. You're gonna have to clean up your own room.'"

Alice Davis

Alice Davis was sitting in the kitchen of her new home in June of 1957, stripping wallpaper. She called her husband, animator Marc Davis, at his office at the Disney Studio, and told him she was too tired to cook dinner and that they should go out instead for a bite. "Fine," Marc said.

Alice and Marc went to the Tam O'Shanter, one of Walt's favorite restaurants and a frequent hangout of the Disney animators and Imagineers. As they were sitting and enjoying their cocktails, Alice saw a hand on her new husband's shoulder. She looked up and said she "almost swallowed her glass"—it was Walt Disney.

"Introduce me to your new wife, Marc," Walt said. He pulled up a chair and joined Marc and Alice for a cocktail, taking an immediate interest in what Alice did for a living. He sat with them for the better part of a half hour, listening and asking questions about Alice's professional career as a clothing and costume designer. He was particularly fascinated by a new type of fabric that Alice was working on, called "elastic." Eventually Walt stood up and said, "Well, I'd better be going." He walked a few steps away before turning back around and looking at Alice and saying, "You know, you're going to work for me someday."

Six years later, Alice was at home and got a call from Walt's secretary. "Alice, Walt wants to know if you'd design the costumes for 'small world'? Yes? Be here at 9:00 tomorrow morning."

Alice went on to design the costumes for "it's a small world" alongside one of her idols, Mary Blair. She designed most of the costumes for the Pirates of the Caribbean, Flight to the Moon, and Walt Disney's Carousel of Progress as well, among others. She and her husband, Marc, were named Disney Legends, were married for more than 50 years, and were apparently the inspiration for Pete Docter when he wrote Carl and Ellie's characters for the Pixar movie, *UP*.

From Alice:

"I get angry reading negative things about Walt. He was a joy to work with and for. There was all kinds of freedom, mentally as well as physically. When I was pressed on small world, I was allowed to come in to work weekends. I didn't have guards looking over me. Meeting Walt and working for him was one of the pleasures of my life. He was the best boss you could have. My husband would agree and said it best: Working for Walt Disney was the best school he ever attended."

The Beginning of "it's a small world"

I asked Rolly Crump what it was like to work for Walt Disney. "Walt came in one day and said, 'You know, there's still one piece of real estate left at the World's Fair,' he said. He said, 'I think we should get that,' and he said, 'I think it should be a little boat ride.' We all kinda looked at each other like, what's he talking about, 'a little boat ride'? We were thinking of something like Storybook Land (Canal Boats) in Disneyland... we thought, 'my God, we're doing all this high tech stuff like Lincoln standing up and talking and he wants to do a 'little boat ride?'. And we thought, well, he's crazy but we'll do whatever he says. Well, what happened was, they asked Marc Davis to do a rendering of what the inside of 'small world' would look like with children dancing and everything and, so, he did a beautiful rendering of what it mighta looked like inside: a tent with little children running around and everything. And the next time we had a meeting with Walt, they showed him that sketch, and Walt said, he took one look at it and he said, 'What's Mary Blair doing?'"

(While Walt Disney wasn't good at giving praise, he also wasn't great at direct criticism or candor. He'd do this often where, if he didn't like what one person came up with, he didn't tell them he didn't like it. Instead, he'd ask for someone else's interpretation of his, Walt's, original idea.)

Rolly: "Now, what it was, was, I think that what he thought of Marc's drawing, it was okay, but Mary Blair was so childlike in her stylizations and so perfect for the idea of this show, so that was it. She was made the original concept designer for the whole show and then the rest of the kids who worked at WED, including myself, copied her work and helped put the whole show together. Meanwhile, Walt said, 'Roland,' he said 'I want you to build me a tower of propellers.' He said, 'I want you to develop the Tower of the Four Winds for me.' So I did. I actually built a half-inch scale model, and all of those propellers on that model spun. And, so, we had a great time with it, and that's how the Tower of the Four Winds came about."

The "it's a small world" Clock

Imagineer Rolly Crump was the one tasked by Walt Disney to design the facade of "it's a small world" when it was brought from the New York World's Fair to Disneyland. He used Mary Blair's artwork as inspiration, but it was Rolly who came up with the overall design. He told me all about it when I had him on my podcast, Turkey Leg talk, a bunch of years ago.

"We're not gonna put a band out there!"

"There was a platform out front and Walt said, 'Well, Rolly, what are you gonna put on there?' And I said I don't know, maybe we'll have bands playing. We'll have a bandstand out there. And he said, 'We're not gonna have a bandstand out there!' He says, 'You know what? Why don't you put a clock out there?' So I said, 'Okay!'

"So I designed a clock and built a model of the clock...and the model I built actually worked. And I had the music with it. So I had a complete show in a model; a half inch model of wood of this clock, and the doors would open up and the little characters came out and everything. And I was thrilled with it. I was absolutely thrilled with it. And we showed it to Walt. There's actually a photo around of Walt and I looking at it and laughing. And he said, basically, 'That's great. I love it. Build it.'

"So, that's where the clock came from. But, again, Walt would come up with just a simple little statement, like, (in a Walt Disney impression) 'Why don't ya put a clock out there?!' and that gave me the key on what to do and then we got finished and it turned out to be gorgeous!"

Rolly, Walt, & the Tower

In 1964, while Rolly Crump, Mary Blair, and others were working on "it's a small world" and getting it ready for the New York World's Fair, Walt Disney came to Rolly and gave him another assignment. He had seen these tiny propellers that Rolly had designed at WED and loved the kinetic nature of them. Walt asked him to design a tower of propellers that would stand outside the "it's a small world" pavilion. As Rolly told me on my podcast, this led to a wonderful "cute story" about Walt.

"Walt came to me and said, 'I want you to design The Tower of the Four Winds for me'. And I did. I built a half inch square model, and every one of those propellers spun, and so we had a great time with it, and that's how the Tower of the Four Winds Came about. Now, this gets back to honesty.

"What happened was we built the Tower of the Four Winds in Los Angeles off of my model that I did. But the engineers made it so heavy and so cumbersome that I really hated it. I really did, I just thought, 'Oh my God, they lost the light and the airiness of the Tower that I wanted to create.' But they went ahead and built it and I looked at it and I was quite, well... like I said, I was upset by it.

"Well, I had to drive Walt down to see, you know, the big tower that was down there at the engineering company. So we got down there and Walt looked at it and then he looked at me and he said, 'Well, what do you think, Rolly?' And I said, 'Well, I think it's a piece of crap!' Well, I don't think anyone ever told Walt that something they had designed was a piece of crap, but I was just being honest with him! And he knew, he knew I was being honest and he said, 'Now Roland,' he said, 'it can't be a piece of crap because it cost me two hundred thousand dollars!'"

The Tower of the Four Winds was eventually disassembled, shipped out to New York, reassembled, and stood in front of "it's a small world" for its entire run at the New York World's Fair.

Walt Disney Surprises Bob Gurr with the Magic Skyway

On my podcast, Turkey Leg Talk, I used to have a segment where listeners could email in a question for Bob Gurr, and he'd answer one question at the start of each show. A few years ago, a listener asked about the background story of the Ford Magic Skyway that Disney and Bob designed for the 1964-1965 New York World's Fair.

"Walt Disney was having one on one meetings with Henry Ford II and other personnel at the Ford Motor Company. Well, they were trying to figure out what to do at the New York World's Fair and they thought that they should hire the Disney Company, who looked like they would be able to do a job like that. Ford was quite confident with what they (the Ford Company) could do with the design of the attraction, while Walt had a completely different idea, and said, 'You should do this.'

"So they discussed the fact that in the 1940 World's Fair, the Ford Motor Company had, you know, Ford and Lincoln and Mercury cars, and drivers would drive guests around on this little track. So that was in the forefront of Henry Ford's thinking, that 'We should make sure our guests have the chance to see and feel and touch Ford Motor Company cars.' And they said, 'Well, it's too expensive to have drivers to try to do that,' and Walt said, 'Well, we'll simply have an automatic conveyance system we design, it's as simple as that.'

"I believe it was Henry Ford who asked Walt Disney, 'Well, how would you do that?' And Walt said, 'Oh, well we have the Matterhorn track where we have these little booster brakes and with these little wheels in the track, and it works very well.' And then there was a Ford unnamed Vice President who was objecting to all of this and when it came time to proceed with the Disney Company or not proceed, Henry Ford said, 'Well, we're gonna do it.' And this guy started to object, and it was very obvious to Walt, it gave him a big chuckle, Henry Ford reached under the table and kicked that man in the shin so bad, that the man, mid-sentence, stopped what he was doing and approved the agreement. That was a technical decision made quickly in a meeting by non-technical people!

"So, Walt comes back and asks me to take a look at this agreement he made (with Ford), and this is right about the end of June of '61. And he said, 'I want you to get stated on moving Ford Motor Company convertibles in a show we're gonna design, and whatever you do you're gonna use little wheels in the track, 'cause that's what I told 'em!' So, anyways, it was very funny that, instead of giving me a chance to figure out, you know, 'what should we do?', well, it had already been decided what we were gonna do and the ball was thrown to me now! (As Walt) 'Go figure this thing out! I've already promised 'em!'"

The Ford Magic Skyway was the one attraction that did not travel back to Disneyland after the World's Fair ended, but pieces of it did! The dinosaurs that were a part of the Magic Skyway have been a part of Primeval World on the Disneyland Railroad for decades!

Bob Gurr and the Magic Skyway

The Ford Magic Skyway is the one World's Fair attraction that didn't make it's way back to Disneyland after the fair ended. Pieces of it did, of course, like the dinosaurs that have resided in Primeval World for the last few decades, but the attraction itself was far too complicated and had too many "moving parts" to make it practical to move.

There were lots of problems and issues getting the attraction up and running. There was one elevator that would take the cars from the ground level up to be installed on the Skyway track on a higher floor. Bob told me about one particular day when the elevator had a pretty significant malfunction.

"Just before we started to run the track, we were moving the convertibles up an elevator from the lower part of the building up to the track. It was kind of a tedious thing and you had to take these car up one at a time.

"Well, while I was looking at the elevator, we had a red Mercury convertible that came up there and as they were attempting to offload it onto the floor, the car was partway on the floor, partway on the elevator, all of a sudden the elevator started going down by itself. Really slowly, you know, maybe like a foot a minute. And, it's slowly crushing the Mercury. You could hear this crashing and banging and glass breaking and the windshield broke. Pretty soon we had the tail end of the car on the floor and the rest of the car in the elevator stuck halfway down to the next floor. We were outta business! We can't put anymore cars in the building and until we chop up and pull that car out and put another elevator in there! So nobody was in a good mood that day! So years later, there was always the joke when we would see the Ford guys again, like, 'Oh, man! Hey, do you remember the red Mercury halfway down the elevator, crunching and cracking?!' Oh boy! There's all this stuff that goes on and these stories that no one's ever heard!"

Bob also told me about how the folks from Ford had literally no faith in Bob and "the Disney people." They thought the system that Bob had designed to move their actual cars through the show would never work, and they didn't hide their surprise when it actually did.

"I think it was the last week of 1963 and the ride was complete and we were starting to load up the cars. And the funniest thing happened. We got enough cars on one track so we could start to do some tests. I was in a spot where I could watch the cars, and the guy started the ride up and all of the cars started moving, and about three minutes later, they stopped. And I heard all this screaming and yelling throughout the building (when the cars were moving), and about three minutes later, it stopped. I had heard all that screaming and yelling and I thought , 'Oh my God, what on Earth happened?!'

"Then Roger (Broggie) grabbed me and he says, 'Come on, we're going over to the hotel next door. We're gonna have a party!' Well it turned out...(laughs) there was a gigantic party with a lot of booze and hors d'oeuvres and everything (that the Ford employees threw). The screaming was, the Ford Motor guys, there were a whole bunch of them there by that time, they were screaming in relief that the thing worked because they did not believe our system would ever work. Can you imagine going to a meeting in which everybody got so drunk because they were so relieved that their neck was not in the noose for going along with the crazy Mickey Mouse Disney guy moving their cars?! And it surprised me because I thought, 'Of course it works! Obviously!' (Laughs) Ohhhh, I'll never forget that drunken party!"

Rolly Crump and the Cave Woman

One of my favorite Rolly Crump and Walt Disney stories is one that he didn't tell me on my podcast, but I read in his book, *It's Kind of a Cute Story*. Rolly was spending time with sculptor Blaine Gibson, who had been working on the human figures for the Ford Magic Skyway attraction that was to go in at the New York World's Fair. Blaine had just finished a cave woman figure that was getting set to be installed, but he didn't feel like he had gotten the skin color exactly right. He asked his pal, Rolly, who was a very athletic, big, muscular guy, especially for the 1960s, to take off his shirt and stand next to the figure so he could compare his actual skin tone with the skin tone of the cave woman figure.

Rolly thought he was kidding at first. But when Blaine insisted, Rolly tore off his shirt, rolled up his pant legs, and started posing with the figure as Blaine started snapping away with his Polaroid camera. Now, the funniest part was, Rolly said that the cave woman was only dressed in a loin cloth around her waist. "She was a large girl. And by large, I mean both in terms of height and endowment. And there was nothing to hide her endowments!"

Rolly grabbed a strip of the fur that the figure's loin cloth was made of and fashioned his own, which he tied around his waist. After a few rather innocent Polaroids, the photos got a little R-rated. "I grabbed the cave girl here, there, everywhere! It was entirely immature, but it was funny to me! Besides, Blaine kept taking shots." Once the session was over, Blaine thanked Rolly, the two had a laugh, then Rolly forgot all about it.

A couple weeks later, Walt came by the office to check with Blaine about something. Blaine told Walt that the answer to his question was most likely in one of the files of Polaroids that he kept on his desk, and now you can see where this is going! Rolly's stomach was in his throat as he heard Walt say, as he was looking over Blaine's shoulder at the Polaroids in the file, "What's THAT? I want to see those."

Blaine explained the reason for the photos, then laid each and every Polaroid out on the table in front of Walt for him to inspect. I'd imagine that the room was spinning for Rolly at that point. He said he was absolutely sure he was going to lose his job. He excused himself, got up from from his desk or table, and then wandered over to the vending machines to grab a soda and try to calm his nerves. He thought he heard Walt stifle a laugh as he was walking away.

A colleague saw Rolly wander away from the meeting and noticed how pale he was. He asked him what had happened. "Walt's looking at those pictures of me and the Cave Girl," he said. "What did he think of them?" his friend asked, his eyes popping out of his head with anticipation. "I think he laughed," responded Rolly.

With that, Rolly felt the presence of someone standing right behind him. He wheeled around and there was Walt. "You're damned right he laughed, Roland!" Walt turned around, walked away, and Rolly worked for Disney for another few decades!

X Atencio, Pirates, and Haunted Mansion

Disney artist and animator Francis Xavier Atencio, known to Disney Fans as X Atencio, worked for Walt from 1938 to 1965. In 1965, Walt Disney told him, "X, it's time for you to move" and he sent him to work at WED (later renamed Walt Disney Imagineering, or WDI) to work on "the pirate ride."

X showed up for work at WED and no one knew what to do with him. He stood around and watched other people work for a few days. Then Walt called WED, got X on the phone, and said, "X, I want you to write the script for Pirates of the Caribbean. There's gonna be scenes with pirates and towns-people and so forth, and there's gonna be a lot of dialogue, and I want you to write it." X was an artist and had never written a script in his life, but Walt told him he knew he could do it and he believed in him. That's how X Atencio became a script writer for Disney's attractions.

Incredibly, this isn't the end of the story! When Walt came to WED to see the mockup of Pirates of the Caribbean, he walked through the models with X, and X told him, "Say, Walt, you know what this Pirate ride needs? It needs a song!" X suggested a melody and even some lyrics and he assumed Walt would have the Sherman Brothers, Richard and Robert, write the song and music. But when Walt heard X's ideas, he said, "Oh, this is good. If you need help writing the music, ask George Bruns to score it." And that, my friends, is how X Atencio, a guy who had never written a script or a lyric in his life, not only wrote the SCRIPT for Pirates of the Caribbean, but wrote the iconic song, "Yo, Ho, Yo, Ho, a Pirates Life For Me"!

Much like Julie Andrews told me on my podcast, Walt just knew how to recognize talent in people. He knew that X was capable of those things and he put him in that position to get uncomfortable and then succeed. Oh, by the way, X also wrote the script for the Haunted Mansion AND the song, "Grim Grinning Ghosts"! You can hear X's voice in a few locations in Disneyland including the skull that tells you to keep your hands and feet inside the boat at all times on Pirates and the skeleton that's screaming "Let me out of here!" from inside the nailed coffin in the Haunted Mansion.

X Atencio. Courtesy Judianne Atencio.

Something Missing in Pirates

One day when construction on Disneyland's Pirates of the Caribbean was nearing completion in 1966, Walt Disney was chatting with some of the Pirates construction crew. Walt learned that one of the workers was from the bayou of Louisiana, and he invited the worker to walk the length of the attraction with him to see what he thought.

The worker and Walt Disney walked through the attraction once, and Walt waited the entire time for a response from the man. None came. Walt asked, "Well, what do you think? Is it realistic? Does it remind you of where you grew up, in the bayou?" The worker said, "It's really good. Something is missing, though. Can we walk through again?"

So this unnamed construction worker walked through Pirates of the Caribbean again, backwards, with Walt Disney.

Pirates of the Caribbean in Disneyland.

They reached the part of the attraction inside the Blue Bayou again with the swamp and the old man playing the banjo on the porch of the shack and the guy snapped his fingers. "That's it! Fireflies! You're missing the fireflies from the swamp back home!" A few days later, electric fireflies were buzzing around Walt's bayou with their lights all aglow.

Doom Buggies Are Candy Apples

Me: "I've read that the Doom Buggy, the vehicle from the Haunted Mansion. I know you came up with it but I read somewhere that you were inspired by a candy apple that was sitting on someone's desk. Is that true?"

Bob: "Oh, that is true! Right after the New York World's Fair... uh, there were some nice attractions at the '64-'65 World's Fair and one of them was a chain of vehicles where people ride in the vehicle (Ford Magic Skyway). If you have a nice chain of vehicles, you don't have to have an anti-collision system and you're gonna have a pretty high (rider) capacity. I was sitting in John Hench's office, you know, just having a casual conversation about, 'Well, what could we do in the future to have a high capacity attraction, a reliable one, and at the same time, tell the story a little bit better?'

"Now, most vehicles up to that time, the seat would be attached to the vehicle, you know whether it's a boat or anything, and you always are facing forward and you look right and left to look at the show. So all you see is the back of the vehicle in front of you and it's only a couple of feet away. So, I picked up this candied apple he had just sitting on his desk and I started twirling it. I said, 'John, what if I took a chain of vehicles on a chassis, and then instead of bolting the seats to the chassis, I'll put a post and then I can rotate the seat part of the body. I can rotate that right and left and, in fact, I could tip it backwards or tip it forwards.'

"So, in other words, we have the ability to yaw right and left and pitch back and forward in the pitch axis. And I says, 'You know, I think the art directors will love this because we could be tellin' a story with a scene on the right side of the car, you know, facing it? And then as we move to the next scene, I could twirl that car really quickly say from the right to the left, even as the chassis is turning, and we could chop quite a few seconds of the segue between scenes. That way, for the same length of an attraction, we can have longer viewing seconds in each one of the scenes.'

"It was so simple! And I said, 'You know, this is a great way to move people.' You know, they could look in all directions. And at that time I was a pilot and one of the things to do with aviation is a radio navigational directional system called omni, or omnirange, with omni meaning 'all'. So I said, 'Yeah, John, it'll be an Omnimover.' So that name got stuck in a few seconds and we've been stuck with it ever since because we've never come up with a trade name for it.

"I started doing that for Monsanto right away for the Adventure Thru Inner Space and then the team that had been working for years on the Haunted Mansion as a walkthrough said, 'Oh, gosh, this will solve the walkthrough dwell problem (higher ups were worried about guests just wandering aimlessly through the Mansion and/or vandalizing it) and we can control the scenes. So now we know what to do.' So, the Haunted Mansion, everybody remembers the Doom Buggy, but they forget that the Monsanto Adventure Thru Inner Space had it first."

Roland, Owen, Orland, or Rolly?

Rolly Crump was on my podcast several years ago and I asked him about moving over from Walt Disney Animation to WED (later Walt Disney Imagineering) and his first time introducing himself to Walt Disney.

"Well, that's a beautiful little story. I was so thrilled to meet him. In fact, when I shook his hand I said, 'Mr. Disney, it's a pleasure to meet with you,' and he said, 'Well, it's nice to have you on board, Roland. By the way, the name is Walt. And don't you forget it,' because he always went with a first-name basis with everyone he dealt with. So that was it!"

In his book, *It's Kind of a Cute Story*, Rolly tells another story about how Walt would always forget his name in the early days, once he first moved over to WED. After a while, Walt started calling Roland Crump "Owen Crump" or just Owen. Rolly didn't know why at first, and he didn't really care! He had the opportunity to work for and with Walt Disney himself, it didn't really matter what Walt called him! He later discovered that Walt had employed a writer named Owen Crump, and that's where the confusion probably started.

After a while, Owen morphed to Orland, and that was poor Rolly's name for weeks. Diane Disney Miller (Walt's daughter), told Rolly that her dad was really bad with names and almost always forgot them. It's why he came up with his own, personal nicknames for the people around him. One morning, Rolly was in a meeting with Walt and Yale Gracey. Walt looked at Yale and said, "Yale, I want you and what's-his-name here to work on the Mansion together." Rolly never took it personally.

Soon after, Walt gave Roland Crump the nickname Rolly and it stuck for the rest of his life. According to his book, when Rolly was a kid he was called Rolly because he was a Junior and his father was Roland, so the nickname was a bit of a full circle moment in his life.

The Famous Pirates of the Caribbean Fireflies

So, where did those awe-inspiring fireflies inside the Blue Bayou Restaurant in Disneyland's Pirates of the Caribbean come from? According to Rolly Crump, Yale Gracey's imagination!

"As we go into the Pirates of the Caribbean ride, I want to talk a little bit about (Imagineer) Yale Gracey. He was the secret to so much of the stuff that we did and I don't think that he ever got his just due, but...if you're in the pirate ride, and you look over in the firefly area when you're in the Blue Bayou, you'll see these little fireflies. And you wonder, 'How in the world they'd do that?'

"Well, what those are, they have what they call a grain of wheat light bulb; it's a little dinky light bulb and it's on a little tiny black cord, and what Yale did was, he took a little piece of black tape and he taped one side of the little light bulb (so one half wouldn't emit light). It was light enough, that if a fan hit it, it would move. So there's this little light bulb on it, but the black tape hides the fact, so you don't see it. So then the fan goes, then you see it, then you don't see it. So here's this little firefly that will go forever, and it's nothing more than a little grain of wheat bulb hanging on a little cord, another one of Yale's magic tricks!"

In the years since, Yale's fireflies have been replaced several times over. When he would see the replacements, Yale would often complain that the new crop of Imagineers didn't stick to his original design.

Yale later admitted that he had never seen a real firefly in his life.

Why Did 'it's a small world' Have Trees on the Roof?

When I asked Rolly Crump what it was like getting Disneyland ready for the arrival of "it's a small world" from the N.Y. World's Fair, he shared this gem.

"Well, here we go again. This is where Walt steps in with an idea that makes everything wonderful. We were bringing 'a small world' back to Disneyland, and the space out front of the building was gonna be about 300 feet long. So what I did was I got the head model builder and he and I sat down with all of the sketches that Mary (Blair) had done, and we traced her sketches. We actually built the whole facade out of cardboard... just black and white ink on white cardboard and we built a half inch square model of the entire facade to show Walt.

"And before Walt came over, we had this tray that had a bunch of trees on it that we were gonna put on the ground in front of 'small world'. And we had it up on a box behind the model of 'small world', so we kept reaching up to take a tree down and put it where we thought we should put it, just because it was quite a ways to reach. That's why we had it up there.

"So, Walt came (to the meeting) early, he came early and there was this bunch of trees up on top of this box that represented the building, and Walt looked at it and he said, 'You know, I really like what you guys did; you have all these trees up on the roof (the way Rolly pronounced it, it rhymed with hoof) of the building, so no one knows there's a building there!' And Fred (Imagineer Fred Joerger) and I just started busting out laughing, and I said 'Yeah, we thought it was a pretty good idea too!'

"And then we kept laughing and he was looking at us like, 'Why are you laughing?' so we told him the real story of why we did it. He said, 'I don't care. It's a good idea anyway!' And that is why the trees were on the 'small world' building there."

Walt Finds His Mary Poppins

Six years ago I chatted with actress Julie Andrews on my podcast. I was told by the Netflix person who set up the interview that I had to talk about ONLY Julie's *Greenroom*, her Netflix show. Never one to 100% listen to authority and instructions, I snuck some Walt and *Mary Poppins* stuff in at the end and Ms. Andrews was wonderful about answering.

Me: "You met Walt Disney when he came to offer you the role of Mary Poppins. Did you know that was going to happen and did you know he was in the audience that night?"

Julie Andrews: "We did know he was in the audience that night but we thought, quite literally, that he was there to see the show, Camelot. Richard Burton was the star of it and I was co-starring with him and the lovely Robert Goulet as well and we thought he had just come to see the show as entertainment and pleasure. But, he asked if he could come backstage afterward and he came into my dressing room and we chatted and then he revealed that he had in mind a film of the books by P.L. Travers, the Mary Poppins books, and would I be interested in coming to Hollywood to hear the songs and see the layout that they had developed for the storyline. I remember thinking, 'Gosh, that sounds wonderful!' But with some dismay I said, 'Mr. Disney, I would love to but I'm afraid I'm pregnant! (Laughs) And I'm about to have a baby...' and he said, 'Well, that's okay! We'll wait!'

He then turned to Tony (Walton), my husband at the time, who was a wonderful theater designer and film designer, and said 'And what do you do, young man?' And Tony explained, and Walt said 'Well, bring your portfolio with you,' which Tony did, and we did go after my time in Camelot was finished. We did go to Hollywood and Walt spoiled us both royally and he hired Tony on the spot when he saw his designs and, of course, Tony got an Academy Award nomination for that. The first film that he had ever done, the first film that I had ever done...and it was the magic of Disney that he just had this talent for, well, for spotting talent, I guess."

Me: "The first movie you did was this little, tiny film called Mary Poppins, right, like this little..."

Julie: "But talk about a quick learning experience!"

Me: "Did you know it was gonna be a huge hit when you were filming it?"

Julie: "Not exactly the hit that it turned out to be. We knew that it was different and unique and charming, you know? Disney's vision was so huge for it to mix animation and live action, it was very new in those days. But, it certainly seemed like it could be successful but I don't think anybody dreamed it could be that big a hit. And how lucky can a girl get?"

Me: "Oh, absolutely! Well, how lucky could we get? That we've gotten to enjoy everything you've done over decades."

Julie: 'Well, it was a great learning experience for me and I will forever be grateful to Disney for that."

The film *Mary Poppins* went on to become the biggest box office draw in the history of the Disney Company. Julie Andrews, in her first film, won the Academy Award for Best Actress. The film was nominated for thirteen Academy Awards, winning five.

Rolly Crump & Walt's Lost Night of Sleep

The late Rolly Crump told me this one about Walt Disney and the early days of working on Disneyland's Haunted Mansion. Rolly is the guy that isn't Walt in this photo.

"I always felt that the Mansion should be scary. Even Walt said, 'People love to be scared.' So I always worked on stuff that was kind of weird, it was different. I saw a film, *Beauty and the Beast*, it was a French made film, and in it it had all these human arms that held torches in the hallway, and then there were human heads that had green steam come out of them, and I thought, 'This is the kind of stuff that should be in the Haunted Mansion.' So I started drawing up all kinds of crazy stuff. I did a Candle Man, a man that was standing there with his hands up in the air and his fingers were all candles. I started developing these crazy characters, and we were gonna give an exhibit of ideas to Walt one day, a group of us, and I had all of my stuff that was kind of weird and my management was a little concerned about Walt seeing the weird stuff so they had me over in the corner with all of my stuff, and everybody else had their presentation right up front.

"So we got finished and Walt said, 'Is that it for today?' and Dick Irvine said 'Yes, that's it.' So then Walt said, 'Well, what's that stuff over in the corner?' And they said, 'Well, that's something that Rolly's been working on.' So Walt said, 'What is it that Rolly's been working on?' and they replied, 'We don't know, why don't you ask him?' So Walt asked me and he and I rolled our chairs over together and I told him exactly what I just told you about the film I saw and how I felt that we should have weird stuff in there, and Walt just said, 'Yeah, but this stuff is REALLY WEIRD!' And I said I know but I just want to do something different. So Walt said, 'How are you gonna use it?' I said I don't know! So we got into this I don't know back and forth and finally he snapped, 'That's it! I'm outta here!' So Walt got up and left and everyone that was in the room came over to me and said, 'See, we told you Walt was wouldn't like it. We knew it was too weird.' I said, I know, I don't know, I was just having fun with it.

"So, the next morning I come into work and Walt Disney is sitting in my chair at my desk at seven o'clock in the morning and the first thing he said to me was, 'You son of a bitch! I didn't get an ounce of sleep last night because of all that weird stuff you showed me yesterday. You know, because I didn't get any sleep, I thought about it all night and I think what we should do is have a Museum of the Weird.' And he said, 'Rolly, you can design all the weird stuff you want and we can tell the public and our guests that you've traveled around the world to find weird things to bring to Disneyland.' And I said, oh, that sounds like a great idea! So Walt had the rest of the guys come in, and he gave them a presentation on the Museum of the Weird using my sketches as the bottom line on it. And when he got finished he said, 'Well, I'm gonna go home and go to bed now' and he left. As soon as he was gone, the other guys turned to me and one of them said, 'See, Rolly! We knew you had something with that weird stuff!'"

Walt died before the completion of the Haunted Mansion and the Museum of the Weird was never built. Many of Rolly's Museum of the Weird ideas did make it into the attraction though, including the arms with the torches, the spinning clock, and more! Unfortunately, Candle Man didn't make the cut BUT a Museum of the Weird comic book was released a number of years ago, honoring the wonderful Rolly Crump!

Walt's Daily Routines

Walt Disney's office at the Disney Studio was made up of three different rooms. The first room was where his secretary, or secretaries, would have their desks and would sit and work. One room was a formal office, where Walt had a piano and would show off some of his miniatures from his collection. The other room was Walt's working office. That was where he took most of his meetings. He had a small kitchen built in in a wall that he could hide with sliding wooden doors when he had company.

Walt would often go to lunch at the studio commissary and the Coral Room, which was sort of a VIP restaurant that he had built when he became a little too famous to be able to enjoy a meal "among the people." He would also eat lunch in his working office, at his desk, often. Normally lunch was simple: a sandwich, a glass of milk, and coffee.

Walt always had coffee on hand and ALWAYS drank it black with no cream or sugar. In the morning, his secretary would leave a piping hot carafe of black coffee on his desk for when he arrived. Normally, he wouldn't even drink much of that first one. He'd pour a cup and forget to or be too busy to drink it. He'd then call his secretary and ask her to pour out the cold coffee and replace it with new, hot coffee. That would go on all morning, according to his secretary Tommie Wilck, who was Walt's secretary from 1958 until his death in 1966.

When he would hold meetings in his office, his secretary would serve black coffee to everyone with no exception. If you were having a meeting during the day with Walt, you were served a cup of coffee. If you didn't drink it, you were to take it with you to go. I guess you had to find cream and/or sugar on your own!

Walt developed a few routines over the years that his secretaries followed each day. The first one was a noon V8 Juice, served to Walt and everyone else who happened to be in Walt's office at that time. No exceptions. If you didn't like it, well, I guess that was tough! That's what Tommie was serving. The second routine was the 12:30 ringing of the lunch bell. Walt had been given this giant bell by the United States Coast Guard as a gift, honoring a film he had made about how icebreaking ships break the ice in the Arctic. One day, Walt's meeting was running about 30 minutes late. He was in a playful mood and Tommie came in and rang the bell, signaling to Walt that it was lunch time. Walt laughed and loved it so much that he asked her to come in each day and ring that bell, letting everyone in the wing know it was lunchtime.

The third routine was the 5:00pm drink. Tommie would pour Walt his favorite, a scotch mist (that was mostly ice), and then would pour whoever else was in the room whatever they wanted. When Walt's days would end at 5, he would normally get back treatment for his old polo injury in his office from studio nurse and friend, Hazel George. In his last years, Walt would invite the Sherman Brothers, Richard and Robert, to his office for his evening tradition. He'd ask them to "Play it." "It" was the song "Feed the Birds" from *Mary Poppins*. It was Walt's favorite. The lyrics really resonated with him. If you don't know what it's about, it's basically a song that says just doing something small can really make a huge difference to someone. When the song would end, according to Robert Sherman, Walt would say, under his breath, "That's what it's all about."

Floyd Norman, Walt, & Praise

Floyd Norman was the first ever African American artist hired by the Disney Company and worked his way through the ranks until he got to work on The Jungle Book with Walt Disney himself. I asked Floyd what it was like working with Walt and how he handled it when his animators did a good job.

Floyd Norman: "He would simply say 'that's good' or 'that'll work' or 'let's move on.' He was not good with praise and accolades. He would acknowledge that you had done your job and that you had delivered what he expected. But, don't expect a lot of glowing praise from the Boss because he wasn't gonna give it. So...Walt saying 'that'll work,' that was high praise indeed. If you got that much from Disney, that was high praise."

Me: "I noticed in your film (*Floyd Norman, An Animated Life*) that when you were working on the scene in *The Jungle Book* with Kaa and Mowgli, that he gave you "Okay, that'll work?""

Floyd: "Yeah! Well, we had shown the sequence to Walt early on and he had seemed pleased with it but he wasn't totally satisfied, and then he decided the reason why he wasn't totally satisfied was that the sequence was good, but it could be better if it had a song. So he had the Sherman Brothers, Robert and Richard Sherman, write a song, "Trust in Me," that was sung by Sterling Holloway (the original voice of Kaa and Winnie the Pooh), and I was there at the recording session when Sterling recorded (singing with a slight lisp) "Truussssssssst in Me." So taking that recording, that song, we went back, Vance Gary (sp) and me, Vance was my partner on *The Jungle Book*, we worked together in the same office...we went back and we redid the sequence to fit with the new song written for us by the Sherman Brothers. Well then, Walt, well, then he was satisfied, and he said, 'Okay, that'll work.'"

Me: "There's your high praise, right there!"

Floyd: "That's all the praise we needed!"

Yale & Rolly Design the Mansion

Rolly Crump told me:

"Yale Gracey and I were hired by Walt to work on the ideas for the Haunted Mansion, 'cause Walt always wanted a haunted mansion in Disneyland. From the day that he opened the park, that was one of the projects that he wanted. So, basically, Yale and I had a great big room that we worked in but we didn't know what we were supposed to do! (Laughs) We were just supposed to come up with ideas that would go into the Mansion.

"Well, luckily, Yale was kind of a Tinker Toy guy and he came up with all kinds of stuff. I didn't come up with anything other than helping him with whatever he wanted. So I built the models for Yale that he wanted to show Walt of the different projects that we were working on. One of them was called Pepper's Ghost. It was a story...well, what it was, was it was an illusion. And there was a piece of glass on a stage, and it was in a book that Yale had. So he wanted me to do this model of Pepper's Ghost, which reflects the ghost into a piece of glass and it looks like he's in your room. So we showed that to Walt.

"And then the next thing we showed to Walt was Yale started taking a projector and projecting it on all kinds of things in the room: on the doorknobs and on the windows and everything. Well, finally, he ended up...he got a looped piece of film, which was 'Mirror, mirror on the wall, who's the fairest one of all,' which was Hans Conried's face, so he projected that on a little Beethoven bust. (Excitedly) And it was absolutely incredible because the little bust looked like it was talking. And when I came back from lunch he had it all set up and showed it to me and I said, 'Oh my God! That's incredible!' Even though the eyes and nose didn't line up, the little sculpture looked like it came to life!

"So we took it to Walt, and Walt just loved it. And, so then we took it and we did it on a larger head at a later date."

Big Al Bertino

You may know that the voice of Big Al from the Country Bear Jamboree was provided by country singer Tex Ritter, but did you know that the name and the appearance for Big Al was based on longtime Disney animator Al Bertino? Al was hired by Disney in 1935 and worked on classics like *Pinocchio* and *Fantasia* before moving over to WED (the early name for Walt Disney Imagineering) where he worked on attractions like Mr. Toad's Wild Ride, the Haunted Mansion, America Sings and, of course, the Country Bear Jamboree.

My all-time favorite Al Bertino story, of course, comes from a time that he was working alongside Walt Disney.

"Walt was working on a Christmas special that would involve Baby Jesus, and came to Al for help. Walt wanted to make sure it was in good taste, so he said, 'Get someone from St. Joseph's Hospital across the street, a nun, and see if she likes it.'

"So I got the mother superior and went through it for her. She said, 'Oh, this is so wonderful, where do you people get your ideas?' Wanting to please her, I rolled my eyes upward and said, 'Well, when we get stuck we get some help from the man upstairs...' and she said, 'Oh, yes, that Mr. Disney is so clever!'"

The quote comes straight from the *South Florida Sun Sentinel*. Big Al does bear a striking resemblance to Al Bertino, if I do say so myself! Pun intended!

Kurt Russell and Walt Disney

Kurt Russell was just a 13-year-old kid, acting in his first Disney film, *Follow Me Boys*, in the spring of 1965. He was also a star baseball player, even at that age, and he and his family already had aspirations of him playing in the big leagues some day. In those days, the movie was being filmed at Disney's Golden Oak Ranch, which was nowhere near the fields where Kurt's baseball games were held. His parents didn't want him missing any games, so they signed a deal with Walt Disney that would allow him to leave the set, by helicopter, every day at 3:00pm.

One Friday afternoon, filming was running late. Director Norman Tokar wanted to get a few more shots before losing Kurt for the day. 'Just three more shots', he commanded. Kurt reminded him that he had to leave; it was actually the day of the championship game for his All Star tournament and he absolutely could not be late. The director kept pushing it. 2:45pm came and went, and Kurt kept anxiously looking at his mom on set, trying to figure out what the heck to do. At 2:59pm, he heard the blades of the helicopter spring to life: "See ya Monday!" Kurt shook the director's hand and he and his mom ran off to their waiting ride to the field. Kurt got the game winning hit that night to win the title.

All weekend, Kurt was sweating it. He had a contract with Walt that said he could leave the set at at 3 o'clock sharp, but he was nervous that Walt would hear that he had disobeyed the director's wishes and he'd be fired. Baseball was his true love but he loved acting too and his dad was spending a lot of money on those helicopter rides.

Kurt got to set that Monday morning, went to makeup and wardrobe, and was on his way to class in the little schoolhouse on set when he noticed Walt about 100 feet away and walking straight at him. He figured he'd better go take his tongue lashing or firing like a man, so he walked straight to him and did not try to avoid him. When he got closer, he noticed that Walt had a huge smile on his face. He laughed as he playfully hit Kurt on the shoulder, "I hear you got the game-winning hit the other night! Way to go!"

Bob Gurr & the WDW Submarine

Every time I talk to Imagineer Bob Gurr, I learn some new nuggets of Disney theme park history. Today we were talking about his work on the *Nautilus* and 20,000 Leagues Under the Sea for Walt Disney World and he shared this story with me about a photo I had seen of him online with some kind of bottle ready to break over the hull of the *Nautilus*.

Bob: "That was August of 1971 and that picture you saw was the Submarine Number 1 coming out of Tampa Ship, the Tampa Shipyard on the 13th of August of 1971. We were under the gun to finish that first boat and get it up to the park, and that was Jack Gladish the guy who was running the plastic shop, he and I were old friends. He said, "Oh, we found a bottle of beer, let's smash it on the side of the boat." The thing was on the trailer and we had a guy from this moving company drive that boat up to Walt Disney World. We had to take all the back roads, and then we had to stop and push telephone wires up so it would clear..."

Me: "NO KIDDING! That's a famous story, Bob! That's been told for a zillion years that..."

Bob: "Yeah!"

Me: "That *Nautilus* going on the flat bed from Tampa to..."

Bob: "Yeah! Well, we couldn't get permits for anything. "Oh, just have a truck go out and with a stick hold them (the wires) up..."

Me: "That's really how they did it, huh?"

Bob: "It was...Florida..."

Me: "Yeah, Florida in 1971!"

Bob: "Yeah! Dick Nunis, the President of Walt Disney World, he threatened us, he said, 'You're gonna deliver that on the 13th!' And I said, 'Yes sir!' So anyway, by the time we pulled up the back roads with the trailer, the trailer was so overloaded that several of the tires had popped and the others were on fire. And we pulled in that last couple of hundred feet and I looked at Dick Nunis and I said, 'Here's your boat!'"

Tony Meets Claude

It was a January day in 1967. Nineteen-year-old Tony Baxter was on a break from scooping ice cream in Disneyland and, like he often did, was wandering around backstage by New Orleans Square and exploring. He took an emergency staircase down to what is now the famous jail scene of the Pirates of the Caribbean attraction, trying to get a better look at the audio animatronic characters and the unfinished scenes.

As he was tiptoeing around, trying not to get noticed by anyone, Tony heard a voice call out from down below, "You can't see very much from up there, why don't you jump down into the canal and I'll give you a tour!" Tony walked down into the still dry canal where the boats of the attraction would eventually go. For the next hour, this gentleman gave a 19 year old Disneyland cast member a tour of the attraction that would change Disney theme parks forever. Tony was docked pay and reprimanded by his boss at Carnation Plaza Gardens, where he was working, but it was worth it! That chance meeting and tour gave Tony all the motivation he needed to go for his ultimate dream of working in Imagineering.

A few years later, Tony was able to land an interview with WED (the previous name for Walt Disney Imagineering), who had an opening in the Model Shop. He took with him the typical college student art portfolio, but also brought along a contraption he had created that he thought might catch the interviewer's eye. When Tony told the interviewer about the contraption, he was asked to bring it into Imagineering and set it up.

For the next few hours, Tony would run his machine, reset it, and run it again. The men and women of Imagineering would come into the room, check it out, then leave. One Imagineer stayed in the room and asked Tony tons of questions about his most recent Disneyland jobs, working on Adventures Thru Inner Space and the Submarine Voyage. Tony didn't recognize that this Imagineer was the same gentleman who had taken him on the tour of the unfinished Pirates years before. It was Claude Coats, who had been close with Walt Disney and had been with the Disney Company since the *Snow White and the Seven Dwarfs* days.

40 Miles Per Hour on the Monorail!

When the Contemporary Resort was nearing completion at the end of the summer in 1971, Bob Gurr was hard at work finishing the Walt Disney World Monorail System. One of my favorite Bob stories comes from that time. The higher ups at Disney just did not believe that a monorail running through a hotel wouldn't cause a disturbance every single time. Bob knew it wouldn't be a problem, but on Labor Day of 1971, he was asked to put his theory to the test.

"A lot of architects and civil engineers, when they think of overhead trains, they think of the Chicago L which is a big rattle trap of a system. They thought that a monorail going through a hotel would cause the same kind of noise and vibration and disruption. They would not believe that a monorail, with the suspension it's got with rubber tires and a very high density concrete beam, there would be no detectable vibrations through the building, but they still wouldn't believe it. This was 1971, pre-opening, and it turned out to be Labor Day, which was the day we could test it while all the workers were home for the holiday. We had a seismograph that I had the company purchase several years before that was used to detect earthquakes. Well, we had been using it for all the vehicles to measure the ride forces. So, we bolted this big ol' box to the concrete deck and I was supposed to drive the train while a couple of people operated the seismograph.

"So the idea was that I would go through the building at wide open power, as fast as the train would go, and I remember coming in from the south side and there's an opening that the train passes through, and I'm going about 42 miles per hour, and I thought, 'That opening is too small!' (Here's where Bob and I both laugh really loud because his delivery of that line killed me!) You're going through the Mouseport, you know? I went through there, and ah! You've never seen such a sight! I went through there, it didn't take more than ten seconds to get the train through the length of the building. And then I hear on the radio, 'Okay, it looks good, but we're not getting any data (on the seismograph), so do it again!'

"So I went around for another lap and did that and it turned out that the seismograph didn't detect anything. But my hair was standing on end at the end of that session! I was the only person on record that ever went faster than 5 miles per hour through that building!"

Bob Gurr's Favorite Attractions

Imagineer Bob Gurr designed many of the iconic Disney theme park attractions and vehicles we know and love. His list includes the Doom Buggies, the Monorails, the Matterhorn, the Submarines and many, many more! A listener of my podcast wrote in and asked Bob a great question a few years ago and I wanted to share his answer with you, because it's really fantastic and I had forgotten all about it until today...

Me: "What was your favorite of the attractions you did work on and do you have a favorite of the attractions that you did not work on?"

Bob: "Yeah, of the ones that I've worked on, my favorite is the fire engine on Main Street. And the one that I didn't...well, I worked on it a little bit...but 'it's small world'.

"The reason for that is of all of the kinds of attractions that go into amusement parks around the world, once you're in a pleasant mood, you wanna have a nice day with your family and your kids. You don't wanna faint, you don't wanna go through the banging and jarring around with the loud racket and a bunch of stuff...just, get on a boat and go into 'small world.'

"To your eye nothing needs to be explained; no words are necessary. They're singin' songs, it doesn't matter what they sing. Just the eye candy of seeing beauty and lightness and color and simplicity and children and things that are kinda fantastical. You're not being bombarded with what we call 'immersive stuff' today. You're not bombarded at all. You're taking a boat ride in a quiet and beautiful place with the people you love. That, to me, is a Walt Disney attraction.

"Now, in the case of the fire engine, it was because I talked him (Walt Disney) into the fire engine and normally he picks everything in the park and I'm the only one (in Walt's day) that got an attraction started that he didn't start. But after we designed it and I built it and I drove it down the freeway and delivered it in 1958, it turns out that Walt wanted a fire engine after all because he was always dragging people around with him—he'd just put 'em all in the fire engine and he'd drive them around!"

Imagineer Bob Gurr.

Bobby & Herbie

Bob Gurr has told me some great stories over the years about the folks he worked with within the Disney Company. One of his favorite guys was Herb Ryman, who just so happened to be one of Walt Disney's favorite guys as well. Walt called him Herbie, so everyone else at the studio started calling him Herbie. Walt was a nickname guy, apparently, and a lot of the men who worked for him were given nicknames. Roland Crump became Rolly, Bob Gurr became Bobby, Richard and Robert Sherman became Dick and Bob, or the Sherman Boys, and Herb Ryman was Herbie.

Bob first met Herb within his first year of working in the WED Machine Shop in 1954 and the two became fast friends. They would often walk the grounds of the studio lot together, where Herb literally knew everyone, since he had been with Walt and his company since 1938. When Walt moved the WED offices a few miles away from the studio, to Glendale, Bob and Herb's new spots were only a few feet from one another. Most WED employees would go out to lunch, but Bob and Herb would brown bag it and hang out in their offices, where Herb would crack Bob up with stories of the Disney Studio past. Bob said it was mostly because he was a fresh set of ears to hear the stories Herb might've told everyone else already, but Bob ate it up!

In his book, *Bob Gurr: Legendary Imagineer*, Bob talks all about their 30+ year friendship. Herb would come to dinner at Bob's family home, and he would always bring a signed print of his latest work. As I mentioned above, everyone went by nicknames. Bob's nickname from Herb was "Glider Gurr," since Bob was a glider pilot. When Bob would visit Herb's office and not find him there, he would lightly sketch a glider in the sky of Herb's current drawing, as a calling card. He told me if anyone else had ever messed with Herb's drawing, there would've been hell to pay.

Herb was extremely independent with his work, according to Bob. No one at the studio ever pressed him on the completion of a project or gave him a deadline. Not even Walt, apparently. "One time, WED design manager Dick Irvine sternly set a finish date. Herbie quietly put on his coat and left, not to return for many days. Great art will be done in its own time. That never happened to Herbie again."

Floyd Norman on Walt & Rolly

One of my favorite topics to talk about when I speak to Disney Legends is their experiences with other Disney Legends. I talked to Floyd Norman, who worked alongside Walt Disney in the 1950s and 1960s about what it was like working with fellow Disney Legend and all around character, the late Rolly Crump.

Floyd: "Rolly was my first boss at Disney. When I was a young kid, the first guy I worked for was Rolly Crump. So Rolly and I go way back."

Me: "I spoke to him once in my life for about two hours), he seems like he was a bit of a wildcard at the studio, was he?"

Floyd: "Oh my! Rolly was, uh...boy, how would you put it? Rolly was the first...well, not the first because there were other odd-balls at Disney. But Roland Crump was unique in that he didn't really fit into a category. He did his own thing. He was his own man. He didn't dress the way the other artists dressed; he didn't behave the way the other artists behaved. He was kind of like this, uh, I guess you could say, for the 1950's, he was part of the counter culture. He was not conservative. He was way out there...he was a progressive. He was unpredictable and yet highly creative. We often had a joke that, uh, Walt Disney, if he had had his way, that Walt Disney wanted to be Rolly Crump. And I think that's why Walt liked Rolly so much."

Me: "Yeah, he was kind of like Walt's alter-ego."

Floyd: "He really was! He really was. And a lot of people were not that happy about Rolly's relationship with the boss. Because Walt really liked Rolly, and Rolly often went against the grain and it sometimes irritated the other Disney artists and the other Imagineers because Rolly was so unique. But that's what made Rolly Crump so special, because he wasn't like everyone else. He was unique. And Walt Disney realized that and that's how Walt found his talent. Walt Disney actually found Rolly Crump in the Disney Studio. Apparently no one else was paying much attention to Rolly Crump and Walt said, 'Who is this guy?' and 'I want him to come work for me.' Of course, he was already working for Disney, but Walt meant on a more personal relationship over at Walt Disney Imagineering."

Me: "Yeah, I'm thinking of a couple of the stories that he told me, and some of them I couldn't put in the podcast because... my podcast is family-friendly so we have to watch it."

Floyd: "Yeah, I know...I know exactly what you mean!"

Me: "He told me a couple and I was like, 'Alright, well I have to edit these!' (Laughing more). And then he told me a couple of stories where there were a couple of colorful words that I had to beep out as well! Yeah, but I just imagine this muscle-bound guy, in a room with all of these skinny animators in the 50's and 60's. He told me a story about driving his motorcycle through the hallways of a building (in the Disney Studio)."

Floyd:" That wouldn't surprise me!...There are so many Rolly (Crump) stories. Picture these Disney artists in their white shirts and ties, you know? And there's Rolly who was wearing a pair of shorts and a Bermuda shirt and sandals. He was totally his own man. He did his own thing. And, he did things his way. And, apparently Walt was okay with that as long as he, as long as Rolly came up with great ideas, Walt Disney was just fine with Rolly Crump."

Waffles With Strawberries

Walt Disney hired people he trusted to do the jobs that he required, and would (pretty reluctantly) fire those who didn't live up to his expectations. Imagineer Bob Gurr told me that if an employee was not working out the way Walt had anticipated he or she would, he would have that employee moved to a building or a room that was far away from the action of the rest of the Disney Studio. Walt would then cut off all mail and calls to that employee. He said that most employees would realize, within the week, that they were no longer needed at the studio and would stop showing up. Bob said It was a way for Walt to fire employees without confrontation, which he preferred over causing a scene.

Lack of effort from his employees drove Walt bananas, of course, but what drove him even more insane were "yes men." Walt really wanted everyone who worked with or for him to share their honest opinions when asked for them, so he did not have patience for those individuals who he thought were telling him what he wanted to hear.

Imagineer Rolly Crump told a story about a time when he went out for a breakfast meeting with Walt and three or four other Disney Studio employees. Rolly said that a waitress came over to the table and asked the first man to her left, a studio employee, what he'd like for breakfast. "Steak and eggs," the guy said. Walt was next up and ordered waffles with strawberries on top. After Walt's order, the first employee said something like, "You know, Walt, that sounds good," and changed his order to waffles with strawberries on top. Then the third employee ordered waffles and strawberries...then the fourth. With that, Walt stood up, threw his napkin onto the middle of the table, let some four letter words fly, and stormed out. That meeting never even got started.

"Sinking" a Submarine

I talk a lot about Imagineer Bob Gurr's work in Disneyland, but Bob did the same kinds of work for Walt Disney World before the grand opening as well! Recently he and I were talking about the construction of the Disneyland submarines, and the conversation shifted to the submarines for 20,000 Leagues Under the Sea in Walt Disney World, then back to Disneyland. After Bob had delivered the first submarine from Tampa Ship to Walt Disney World in 1971, it was Bob who was tasked with figuring out how to get the submarines to "submerge."

Bob: "Oh, and then I thought I was done with it (the submarine design and construction) but Dick (Nunis) said, 'No, no no. The company that designed the boat, Morgan Yacht, we took the job out from under them and gave it to Tampa Ship, and we're too busy with the railroad. You're gonna figure out how much lead goes where so the boat sinks to the proper level."

Me: "Oh, gosh. So you had to do all of that yourself?"

Bob: (sighs and comically responds quietly) "Yeah...So, I had to go get the drawings of the hull from Morgan Yacht to calculate volume, and water's sixty three pounds a cubic foot (laughs)...I had to do some calculations in one morning, because we had already ordered tons of lead. I mean, there was lead pig (lead containers sometimes used for weighing things down), ahhh, everywhere! And I got a crew, so I've got a whole bunch of guys picking up lead pig and, ya know, that stuff weighs like forty five pounds a piece. So, I figured out where the lead goes and how much. It took about a day and I kept on watching the boat going down and watching the water level and then at one point it was like, 'Oh! I got it!'

Me: "That's awesome! So, was it you that came up with the idea for the bubbles, first in the Disneyland version? It's something else I read recently in a book, that someone was saying that it had to go down lower, and then someone else said, 'Why don't you just add bubbles outside the portholes to make it look like you're going down lower?' Was that you that suggested that?"

Bob: "No, no no. Admiral Fowler, if we're gonna do something, he's a boat guy. Okay, he's got his nose in all the boats, like Roger (Broggie) has his nose in all the steam trains. Okay. So, anyway, Fowler and I started this in March of '58. So he says, 'We've got to have it go down about three feet.' So I did a bunch of studies to figure out about how to get a submarine to go up and down. And then, uh, he said, 'Also, we want to have an underwater cable drive.' Okay...he's issuing orders. Okay... (Admiral Fowler was a Navy guy and a real admiral who oversaw the building of warships in many, many shipyards during WWII.)

"So, concurrently, Roger (Broggie) and I went up to San Francisco. We call a guy up there that runs the cableway in

*The Mariner submarine about to "dive," with
Matterhorn Mountain in the background.*

San Francisco. So, we go up and spend the day with this guy and he's telling us, 'I want to show you why you'd never wanna use cables for anything.'

"So, we came back to tell Joe (Fowler), 'No. That won't work.' Okay, now what are you gonna do? Okay, we'll take a propeller and stick a motor in it, okay. And in the meantime, we have a test tank out on the studio lot, testing special effects. And somebody...nobody knows who it was...says, (in a dull, slow voice), 'Well, if you just had some bubbles coming up when it starts to move, you'd think you're sinkin'."

Me: "And that's how it happened?!"

Bob: "Just like that!"

Me: "That's funny, man!"

Bob: "So we put an air hose in the test tank and looked out the portholes.'Oh yeah! They'll never know we're not sinkin'!"

Flying on *The Mouse*

In January of 1966, Walt Disney asked several of his top men to join him on a trip to Pittsburgh, PA on his private plane to visit the Westinghouse Company. Westinghouse had just built a demonstration of an advanced automated transit system, called Skybus, and Walt was interested in seeing if the technology would fit in his new Experimental Prototype Community of Tomorrow, or EPCOT. Walt was also interested in showing off his plans for the new city and he wanted Westinghouse to put together a proposal for an all new electrical system for the Disneyland Monorail. Bob Gurr was one of the seven Walt asked to join him for the trip, and he told me all about it on a podcast a few years ago.

Apparently after touring the Westinghouse facilities and riding on the demonstration Skybus, the Westinghouse guys, as Bob called them, took the Disney guys, including Walt, to lunch for lobster salad. They wanted to know all about Walt's latest movies and asked him a ton of questions about how the industry worked. They were particularly interested in how Walt got his footage for the True Life Adventure series of films, and if all of the footage that was recorded was used in the films. Walt told a pretty off-color story about the personal relationships of some of those wild animals...that's the best way I can say it where you can still tell this to your kids! The personal lives of those animals was WAY too much for kids to see, so Walt said that footage would remain in the Disney Vault. Bob said that Walt had the whole room cracking up!

When Walt and his crew returned to their hotel after lunch, Walt wandered over to the hotel gift shop. He noticed that all of the Disney toys and merchandise were on a bottom shelf. He looked at Bob and the others and said, 'C'mon, boys!' And he and the other guys moved all of the Disney stuff to the top shelf, moving what was up there to the bottom shelf. Just then, the cashier of the gift shop walked over. "MAY I HELP YOU?," she asked. "Nope, we're almost done here," Walt told her.

Walt then walked over to the lunch counter and asked the boys to join him for a cheeseburger and a malt (he had just eaten; Bob said it puzzled him too). Unfortunately for Bob, he didn't get included in that invitation. "Bobby, you're too fat," Walt said. Bob didn't mind. He said that he was "very plump in those days and certainly didn't need a second lunch."

I think that's 7 too many passengers!

Roy O. Disney:
The Guy Behind the Guy

Many of us have heard stories or have read about the creation of Disneyland. Walt Disney came up with the idea for a theme park, "a family park where parents and children could have fun – together," while sitting on a park bench in Los Angeles' Griffith Park and watching his young daughters ride the carousel. Walt Disney was the creative visionary and the driving force behind much of the Disney Company's success in it's early days. What many people haven't heard, however, is that Walt's older brother, Roy O. Disney, was just as instrumental (or even more so) in getting things done than Walt. When Walt Disney would come up with some outlandish new idea, it was Roy who (after telling his brother it was impossible) was taxed with coming up with the money for the new project. Snow White & the Seven Dwarfs, Disneyland, and certainly Walt Disney World never would have been created if not for Walt's less-famous sibling. Let's take a look at Roy O. Disney, The Guy Behind The Guy.

Roy O. Disney was born on June 24, 1893 in Chicago, Illinois. As a child, he and his younger brother Walt learned about hard work and dedication from their father, Elias Disney, who purchased a newspaper route in Kansas City, Missouri (where the family then lived) in 1911. Elias put his sons to work each and every day. They'd deliver more than 700 newspapers in the morning before school, then another 600 in the evening (and I complained when my parents made me get a job bagging groceries at 16!) Elias was a tough customer who in this day and age wouldn't be looked kindly upon as a father, often handing out physical punishment when his sons disobeyed orders. It was because of Elias's actions and parenting that Roy told Walt one evening in 1912 that he was leaving and never coming back. The next morning when Walt woke up, Roy was gone.

Roy O. Disney took a job as a bank teller in 1912 and then later joined the Navy in 1917 when he learned that the United States was about to enter World War I. After a few years in the Navy, Roy wound up in a Veteran's Hospital in 1923 battling a case of tuberculosis. Walt came to his bedside with an offer from cartoon producer Margaret J.Winkler (along with $40 in his pocket). The brothers signed a deal with Winkler for six episodes of a combination of animation and live action called The Alice Comedies, and the Disney Brothers Studio was born.

In the early 1930s, Walt Disney came to his older brother Roy with a crazy new idea. Mickey Mouse had become a money-making machine for the Disney brothers and their studio, and Walt wanted to take advantage of that. He believed that due to the popularity of animation and Mickey Mouse, he could create and produce a full-length animated feature film. Roy originally wanted no part of the idea and constantly tried to talk Walt out of even trying to get the finances together, but finally broke down and agreed thanks to the enthusiasm and confidence of his younger brother. Walt convinced Roy that he could produce Snow White and the Seven Dwarfs for about $250,000. It was Roy's job to constantly travel to and from New York City to visit the offices of the Bank of America to ask for more and more money to help complete the film. Although Roy was successful in raising the majority of the cash, in the end Walt Disney even had to mortgage his own Los Angeles home in order to finance the film which ended up costing $1,488,422.74! Roy's trust in his brother paid off in the end, and Snow White and the Seven Dwarfs, which was being called "Disney's Folly" by the press, ended up becoming one of the most commercially successful films of all time.

In the early 1950s when Walt again came to Roy and told him about his ideas for Disneyland, Roy told Walt he was crazy. Even Lillian Disney, Walt's wife, backed Roy and said the idea would never work. Walt Disney was as determined as ever and eventually talked his brother into yet another project that was way over their heads and WAY more expensive than they could afford. It was again Roy who had to go to New York City to explain to investors exactly what his younger brother was trying to accomplish with his new "theme park." He eventually signed a contract with ABC where the Disney company would produce a weekly television show titled "Disneyland" and ABC would help finance the park. When Disneyland eventually opened with great success, Roy O. Disney bought out all of the other shareholders who had helped finance the park and by 1960 the Disney Company became the sole owner of Disneyland.

After Walt Disney's death in 1966, Roy decided to march forward with the Florida Project, which was then being called "Disneyworld." Roy came out of retirement to head up the project and ultimately decided to rename the Vacation Capital of the World "Walt Disney World" to honor the vision and dream of his late brother. Roy O. Disney gave the dedication speech at the Magic Kingdom on October 25, 1971 with Walt's greatest creation, Mickey Mouse, by his side.

"Walt Disney World is tribute to the philosophy and life of Walter Elias Disney ... and to the talents, the dedication, and the loyalty of the entire Disney organization that made Walt Disney's dream come true. May Walt Disney World bring Joy and Inspiration and New Knowledge to all who come to this happy place ... a Magic Kingdom where the young at heart of all ages can laugh and play and learn – together."

Roy O. Disney, maybe with the understanding that he and his brother's work would go on to live forever, passed away on December 20, 1971, only a couple of months after the successful opening of Walt Disney World. Although he remains the lesser-known of the founders of the old Disney Brothers Studio, Roy will always be remembered as the man behind one of the most influential men of a generation. Without Roy, Walt Disney would never have been able to achieve all of his dreams and we may not have had all of the wonderful worlds of the Disney company that we do today.

Roy's legacy lives on in Walt Disney World, and he is honored in two very special tributes in the Magic Kingdom. In town square sits a bench with a sculpture of Roy and Minnie Mouse, and along Main Street, USA is a window featuring the Dreamers & Doers Development Co. that reads "If we can dream it – We Can Do It!" Roy O. Disney.

"Walt Disney Was Not a Perfect Man"

There are a lot of misconceptions out there about Walt Disney, and I didn't really understand how many people believed those misconceptions until I started sharing things I wrote in different places, not just here on my FB page. There have been some unfavorable depictions of Walt, the man, in books and on the internet for years. Stories have called him a racist, an antisemite, and a misogynist. I wanted to share a bit of my chat with animator Floyd Norman, who was the first full-time African-American animator employed by the Walt Disney Studio, and who actually worked for and was in those story rooms with Walt.

"Yeah, I think it's the old thing of, you know, people like to tear down heroes. Walt was such a unique individual, such an exceptional gentleman, people often say, 'Well, that's too good to be true. It sounds like an American fairytale.' Like, 'He couldn't have been that good. He couldn't have been that nice. He couldn't have been that smart.' Uh, he couldn't be all those things so they look for flaws and they look for imperfections.

"Now, Walt Disney was well aware he was not by any means a perfect man. You know, he'd be the first to tell you that. That being said, he was not all of the things he's been accused of. He was not a racist. He was not an antisemite. He was not against women...and the the kind of person who would prevent a woman from rising to the top. He was certainly a man of his time who lived in the world of his time, but Walt was exceptional in many ways because, in so many ways and this might surprise people, in many ways, Walt Disney was really a progressive. He gave opportunities to women that few other studios ever did. When I was working in Disney's commercial division, I was working for a woman. Phyllis Hurrell was the head of the film division at the Walt Disney Studios back in the 1950s when I dare say no other major motion picture studio had a woman in charge of a film division. And Walt was the one who put her in that position.

"So, Walt was the type of guy who gave opportunities to people who were qualified. If you could do the job, then the job was yours. It didn't matter who or what you were. What mattered was: were you good? Could you deliver? Could ya do the job? And if you could do that, then Walt Disney was gonna give you every opportunity to excel and to do your best. So, he was a good guy. And it's difficult for me to find negative things to say about him.

"And I've often spent many hours talking to Walt Disney's daughter, the late Diane Disney Miller. I would spend hours talking with Diane about her father when I would visit her up in Napa Valley...and I was happy that I could honestly say that I enjoyed working for her dad and that he was a good guy who treated all people well...and he treated all people respectfully and, uh, I just have nothing bad to say about Walt Disney."

"This box was always on Dad's dresser. In it he just kept things-the little odds and ends that had some sentimental value to him-commemorative pins, a key chain, money clips, pencils and a drawing by his grandson, Christopher. Dad was a baseball fan, and Gene Autry had asked him to serve on the advisory board f the Los Angeles Angels. He was proud of that. Mother gave this box to Walter (Diane's son) some years after dad died."- Diane Disney Miller from the Walt Disney Family Museum.

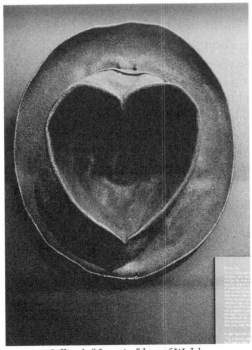

Lillian's "favorite" hat of Walt's,
bronzed by Walt to last forever.

Walt Disney: The Ultimate Gag Man

Walt Disney was the ultimate gag man, always looking for the laugh in any situation. There are several examples of the jokes he played throughout the Walt Disney Family Museum, but this one is my favorite.

Diane Disney Miller was Walt and Lillian Disney's older daughter and the individual who was most responsible for getting the Family Museum built. Her words are all over that place, explaining the meaning behind all of the things you see while you walk through. You can kind of see her words in the photo. She explains that her dad was a sharp dresser in the 1920s and 1930s and his hats always looked good with his clothes. As he got older, though, the hat just became something to stick on top of his head, and it drove his wife, Lilly, crazy!

At some point in the 1940s, Walt and Lilly were at a bull fight in Barcelona and, at the end when all of the attendees would throw their hats into the ring, Lilly tried to grab Walt's old hat off his head and throw it in! Walt caught it just in time, but I guess the message was sent. Of course, being the gag man that he was, Walt held onto the hat, had it bronzed into the shape of a heart, filled it with violets, and gave it as a gift to Lillian on her birthday on February 15!

Acknowledgments

My first thank you goes to my wife, Amy. Your absolute confidence in me, especially when I'm not confident in myself, is why this book exists.

Thank you to my kids Alexa, Zoey, and Jack, for being the first audience for each story and telling me what works and what doesn't. I'm so grateful to be your dad.

Thank you to my Mom and Dad, Patty and Chick, for instilling the love of reading in me before I could even talk. "Wanna read a book?"

Thank you to my brother and sister, Shawn and Lou, for listening to all of these stories 20+ years ago as we walked through the Disney Parks as teens and twenty-somethings. Even if you were bored, you never acted like it!

Thank you to Bob Gurr for setting aside so many hours over the years to talk about Walt. Drinking a Stella and eating Hawaiian pizza while watching the sun set over the hills in your backyard and listening to your stories about your old boss that aren't in the history books was a surreal moment in my life.

Thank you to the Disney Legends who knew and worked with Walt who helped contribute to this book via interviews. Thank you Floyd Norman, Julie Andrews, and the late Rolly Crump. Listening to all of these stories from you was incredible. I still pinch myself.

Thank you to the established authors who have helped me along the way, including Jim Denney, Pat Williams, and Marcy Carriker Smothers. Your love of Walt inspired me to write this Walt book.

Thank you to my editor and publisher, Bob McLain of Theme Park Press. I got a lot of "no's" before, Bob, and your "yes" means the world to me!

Thank you to my friends, Mike L., Pat G., & Derek H. for all of your help and advice over the years with this book and also with my businesses. Thank you for believing in me.

Thank you to my father-in-law, Peter Leavitt, for the total excitement you expressed every single time I called you with a book update. You were one of my favorite calls.

Thank you to my sister-in-law, Karen, for the endless support, help and advice, for, always believing in me, and always listening to my crazy stories and laughing at my (funny?) jokes!

Thank you to those who have contributed to the stories that I've told in the book via social media comments, including Peggy Matthews Rose, John Kuri, and Tom Morris. Thank you Carmen G., for saying I was a writer. I didn't believe it. Thank you to those who sent me photos that I used for the book, including Bill Cohen, Britt Kreutzer, David Gould, Julia Buzard, and Rebecca Johnson.

Thank you to all of the agents on the Ear To There Travel team for your endless support of me and what I do. I am so lucky to have the best group of agents in the Disney travel business! Thank you to all of my readers on Facebook and to all of the listeners of the Ear To There Disney Podcast, now known as Turkey Leg Talk, over the years. Your comments and support was what helped give me the confidence to write this thing.

Thank you, the reader, for taking the time to read these stories that I wrote and put together. I can't believe you did! It's surreal, it really is! THANK YOU!

Lastly, thank you to Walt Disney for being a person so admired that people are still writing books about you more than a half a century after your death. The deeper one digs into your life, the more gems they find. Thanks, Walt.

Bibliography

Barrier, M. (2008). *The Animated Man: A Life of Walt Disney.* Univ of California Press.

Bossert, D. A. (2021). *Claude Coats, Walt Disney's Imagineer: The Making of Disneyland, from Toad Hall to the Haunted Mansion and Beyond.*

Broggie, M. (1997). *Walt Disney's Railroad Story: The Small-Scale Fascination That Led to a Full-Scale kingdom.*

Crump, R., & Heimbuch, J. (2012). *It's Kind of a Cute Story.* Theme Park Press.

Denny, j. (2017). "Nothing Has to Die: The Walt Disney-Ray Bradbury Friendship." www.waltdisney.org.

Denney, J. (2017). *Walt's Disneyland: It's Still There If You Know Where to Look.* Createspace Independent Publishing Platform.

Ghez, D. (2005). *Walt's People: Talking Disney With the Artists Who Knew Him.* Theme Park Press.

Ghez, D. (2005b). *Walt's People, Volume 2: Talking Disney With the Artists Who Knew Him.* Theme Park Press.

Ghez, D. (2008). *Walt's People, Volume 6: Talking Disney With the Artists Who Knew Him.* Theme Park Press.

Ghez, D. (2017). *Walt's People, Volume 10*: Talking Disney With the Artists Who Knew Him. Theme Park Press.

Ghez, D. (2012). *Walt's People, Volume 12: Talking Disney With the Artists Who Knew Him.* Theme Park Press.

Gurr, B. (2019). *Bob Gurr: Legendary Imagineer: Life and Times - Disney and Beyond.* Independently Published.

Gramlich, P. (2016 - 2024). Turkey Leg Talk Podcast.

Iwerks, L. (2022). *The Imagineering Story: The Official Biography of Walt Disney Imagineering.* Disney Editions.

Korkis, J. (2017). *Call Me Walt: Everything You Never Knew about Walt Disney.* Theme Park Press.

Korkis, J. (2010b). *The Vault of Walt.* Theme Park Press.

Korkis, J. (2013). *The Vault of Walt: MORE Unofficial, Unauthorized, Uncensored Disney Stories Never Told: Volume 2.* Theme Park Press.

Korkis, J., McLain, B., & Ghez, D. (2014). *The Vault of Walt: Even More Unofficial Disney Stories Never Told: Volume 3.* Theme Park Press.

Korkis, J. (2016). *The Vault of Walt: Additional Unofficial Disney Stories Never Told: Volume 5.* Theme Park Press.

Korkis, J. (2017b). *The Vault of Walt: Other Unofficial Disney Stories Never Told: Volume 6*. Theme Park Press.

Korkis, J. (2018). *The Vault of Walt Volume 7: Yuletide Tales of Walt Disney, Disney Theme Parks, Cartoons and More: Christmas Edition*. Theme Park Press.

Kurtti, J. (1996). *Since the World Began: Walt Disney World, the First 25 Years*. Disney Editions.

Norman, F. (2013). *Animated Life: A Lifetime of Tips, Tricks, and Stories from a Disney Legend*. Taylor & Francis.

Sklar, M. (2013). *Dream It! Do It!: My Half-Century Creating Disney's Magic Kingdoms*. Disney Electronic Content.

Smith, D. (2012). *Disney Trivia from the Vault: Secrets Revealed and Questions Answered*. Disney Electronic Content.

Smith, D. (2016). *Disney Facts Revealed: Answers to Fans' Curious Questions*. Disney Editions.

Smothers, M. C. (2017). *Eat like Walt: The Wonderful World of Disney Food*. Disney Editions.

Smothers, M. (2021). *Walt's Disneyland: A Walk in the Park with Walt Disney*. Disney Editions.

Susanin, T. S. (2011). *Walt before Mickey: Disney's Early Years, 1919-1928*. Univ. Press of Mississippi.

Thomas, B. (2016). *Magician of the Movies: The Life of Walt Disney*. Theme Park Press.

Thomas, B. (2023). *Walt Disney: An American Original* (Commemorative Edition). Disney Editions. (Original work published 1976)

Williams, P., & Denney, J. (2004). *How to Be Like Walt: Capturing the Disney Magic Every Day of Your Life*. Health Communications, Inc.

Williams, P., & Denney, J. (2019). *Lead like Walt: Discover Walt Disney's Magical Approach to Building Successful Organizations*. Simon and Schuster.

90923942R00105